Southern Living
Party
Cookbook

party in style

Here are three of our favorite accessories for entertaining. To see more products and to contact a local consultant, visit southernlivingathome.com.

Watercolor Vase

Astoria Flatware Caddy

Dress-Me-Up Plate

Southern Living Party Cookbook

SOUTHERN LIVING

EDITOR IN CHIEF	John Alex Floyd, Jr.
MANAGING EDITOR	Clay Nordan
EXECUTIVE EDITORS	Derick Belden, Scott Jones, Warner McGowin, Dianne Young
DEPUTY EDITOR	Kenner Patton
ART DIRECTOR	Craig Smith
CREATIVE DEVELOPMENT DIRECTOR	Valerie Fraser Luesse
PHOTOGRAPHY AND COVER ART DIRECTOR	Jon Thompson
FOODS EDITOR	Shannon Sliter Satterwhite
ASSOCIATE FOODS EDITORS	Shirley Harrington, Kate Nicholson, Mary Allen Perry, Vicki Poellnitz
TEST KITCHENS DIRECTOR	Lyda H. Jones
ASSISTANT TEST KITCHENS DIRECTOR	James Schend
TEST KITCHENS SPECIALIST/FOOD STYLING	Vanessa McNeil Rocchio
TEST KITCHENS PROFESSIONALS	Rebecca Kracke Gordon, Pam Lolley, Angela Sellers
SENIOR PHOTOGRAPHERS	Ralph Anderson, Jim Bathie, Van Chaplin, Joseph De Sciose, Art Meripol, John O'Hagan, Mark Sandlin, Charles Walton IV
PHOTOGRAPHERS	Mary Margaret Chambliss, Gary Clark, Tina Cornett, William Dickey, Beth Dreiling, Laurey W. Glenn, Brit Huckabay, Meg McKinney
SENIOR PHOTO STYLISTS	Kay Clarke, Buffy Hargett
PHOTO STYLISTS	Alan Henderson, Rose Nguyen, Lisa Powell Bailey, Cari South

OXMOOR HOUSE, INC.

EDITOR IN CHIEF	Nancy Fitzpatrick Wyatt
EXECUTIVE EDITOR	Susan Carlisle Payne
COPY CHIEF	Allison Long Lowery
EDITOR	Jane Gentry
DESIGNER	Donna Sophronia-Sims
CONTRIBUTING DESIGNER	Rita Yerby
COPY EDITORS	Donna Baldone, L. Amanda Owens
EDITORIAL ASSISTANTS	Shannon Friedmann, Brigette Gaucher
EDITORIAL INTERN	Ashley Wells
VP, PUBLISHER	Brian Carnahan
DIRECTOR OF PRODUCTION	Laura Lockhart
SENIOR PRODUCTION MANAGER	Greg Amason
PRODUCTION ASSISTANT	Faye Porter Bonner

SOUTHERN LIVING AT HOME

SENIOR VICE PRESIDENT, EXECUTIVE DIRECTOR	Dianne Mooney
DIRECTOR OF BRAND MANAGEMENT	Gary Wright
RESEARCH MANAGER	Jon Williams

EDITORIAL CONTRIBUTORS: Amanda Leigh Abbett, Ginny P. Allen, Lisa Allison, Jean M. Allsopp, Amber Ballew, Adam Barnes, Cindy Manning Barr, Emily C. Beaumont, Ben Brown, Robbie Caponetto, Catherine Carr, Melanie J. Clarke, Missie Neville Crawford, Colleen Duffley, Tracy Duncan, Roger Foley, Trinda Gage, J. Savage Gibson, Jacqueline Giovanelli, Kate Greer, Ann Nathews Griffin, Eleanor Griffin, Mary Lyn H. Jenkins, Sarah Jernigan, Alison Lewis, Lisa Dawn Love, Vince Lupo, Laura Martin, Melanie Parker, Howard L. Puckett, Allen Rokach, Ellen Ruoff Riley, Lacy Kerr Robinson, Karim Shamsi-Basha, Leslie Byars Simpson, Blake Sims, Kim Sunée, Ben Van Hook, Roseanna Whiteside, Amy Jo Young

welcome

Dear Friends,

Gathering with friends and family can be one of life's greatest joys, especially when a cozy atmosphere and delicious food are part of the occasion. Whatever time of year you plan a get-together, let *Southern Living* **At HOME®** help you with this complete guide to entertaining.

Whether you're a first-time hostess or an experienced cook, try our tips for successful entertaining; menus for tasty brunches, lunches, dinners, and picnics; and ideas for stylish presentations for all seasons.

Look inside and you'll find **over 15 menus** for different events, including a birthday party spread, a Fourth of July picnic, and a make-ahead supper club meal. **Prep and cook times** are listed with each recipe, taking the guesswork out of party planning. There's a special bonus section on party planners' tips and tricks (page 104). Learn how to stock the ideal **party pantry,** plan for flawless buffet-style entertaining, and decorate with ease. Use our clever storage ideas to have everything you need at your fingertips. Start the fun now with a few of our editors' favorites:

- *Week at the Beach* offers recipes for five days of fun-in-the-sun meals and a handy grocery list to help you get started (page 64).
- If gardens and fresh herbs are your passion, explore Lucinda Hutson's **fiesta recipes** (page 54). Garden Sangría and Roasted Red Pepper Salsa are a sampling of recipes that show off her Southern charm and her love of Hispanic culture.

- As fall gets under way, learn how to *Tailgate Like a Pro* with first-string recipes such as Most Valuable Cookies and Cream Cheese Rollups (page 80).
- Have a devilishly good time at Halloween with *Goblins Are Gathering* (page 74). A "spooktacular" menu awaits, and decorating ideas from invitations to centerpieces will put you in the spirit.
- By the time the holidays roll around, you'll be a seasoned hostess. Small bites for an appetizer party, make-ahead dishes for a **Christmas brunch,** and comforting Kwanzaa recipes are sure to become year-round favorites, all starting on page 84.

Whether you're ready to spread out the newspaper for a crawfish boil or light the candles for an elegant supper club gathering, you'll entertain with confidence and ease with these **tips, strategies, and recipes** in hand. So relax, keep it simple, and remember it's party time!

Enjoy!

The Editors

on the cover: Broiled Yellow Tomatoes, Steamed Asparagus and Green Beans With Fresh Lemon-Basil Dip, Chicken Tetrazzini, Lemon Muffins, and Garden Salad make a stunning menu for "A Garden Party Trimmed in White" starting on page 12.

contents

Spring

18

54

Summer

Fall

68

88

Winter

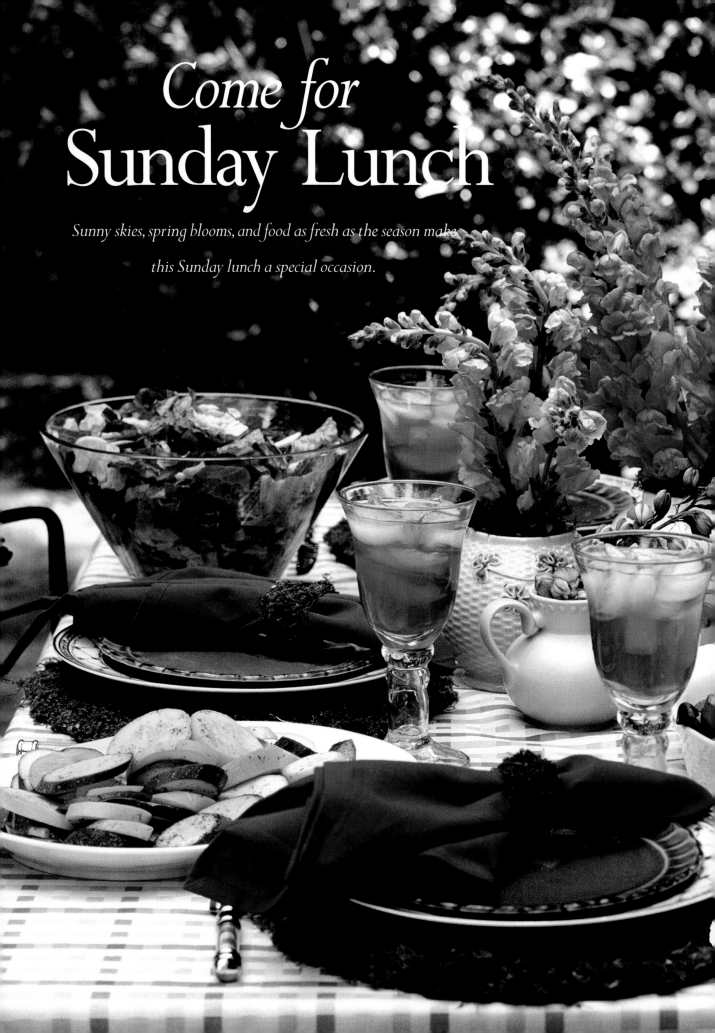

Come for Sunday Lunch

Sunny skies, spring blooms, and food as fresh as the season make

this Sunday lunch a special occasion.

Spring in the South welcomes back sunny weather and gardens in full bloom. Make plans to capture the spirit and host a spring lunch for the family maybe after church on Sunday or to honor mom on Mother's Day. Serve a menu and set a table that blend the old with the new. For starters, update a roasted chicken with Greek seasonings. Then mix passed-down china with new pottery. Serve outside and enjoy an afternoon of talking over old times and creating new memories.

Shirley Harrington

A Sunday Afternoon Lunch
Serves 6

Apricot Bellinis and Iced tea

Romaine Salad With Raspberry
Salad Dressing

Greek Roasted Chicken With Rosemary Potatoes

Sautéed Zucchini and Yellow Squash

or

Mixed green salad

Rolls or breadsticks

Banana-Chocolate Chip Cupcakes With
Peanut Butter-Fudge Frosting

Lemon Tartlets

Apricot Bellinis
MAKES 4 CUPS
PREP: 10 MIN.

6 fresh apricots, halved (about ½ pound)*
1 (11-ounce) can apricot nectar
¼ cup sugar
1½ cups Champagne**
Crushed ice
Garnishes: fresh apricot slices, fresh mint
  sprigs

PROCESS first 3 ingredients in a blender until smooth, stopping to scrape down sides. Stir in Champagne, and serve immediately over crushed ice. Garnish, if desired.
*1 (17-ounce) can apricot halves, drained, may be substituted for fresh.
**1 (12-ounce) can ginger ale may be substituted for Champagne.

The eye-catching colors of raspberry red and grass green are clever choices for this spring table setting. (above) Before lunch, sip on Apricot Bellinis—a refreshing blender drink of apricots and Champagne.

Romaine Salad With Raspberry Salad Dressing

MAKES 6 SERVINGS
PREP: 20 MIN.

For a more subtle onion flavor, soak slices in water 30 minutes, drain, and pat dry with paper towels. Toast a small amount of pecans in a skillet over medium-high heat 2 to 3 minutes, or just until the nuts are warm to the touch. (Be sure not to let nuts overbrown.) As pecans cool, they'll continue to develop the toasted flavor.

1 head romaine lettuce, torn
1 small red onion, sliced
4 ounces crumbled feta cheese
½ cup chopped toasted pecans
4 bacon slices, cooked and crumbled
Raspberry Salad Dressing

PLACE first 5 ingredients in a large bowl, and toss. Drizzle with Raspberry Salad Dressing just before serving.

Raspberry Salad Dressing:

MAKES ABOUT 2 CUPS
PREP: 5 MIN.

1 (10-ounce) jar seedless raspberry fruit spread or preserves
½ cup seasoned rice wine vinegar
¼ cup olive oil

MICROWAVE raspberry spread in a microwave-safe bowl at LOW (30%) power 1 minute or until melted. Whisk in vinegar and olive oil until blended; let cool. Serve at room temperature.

Greek Roasted Chicken With Rosemary Potatoes

MAKES 6 SERVINGS
PREP: 20 MIN.; BAKE: 1 HR., 15 MIN.; STAND: 10 MIN.

See Cook's Notes on the next page for roasting tips.

2 tablespoons Greek seasoning
2 tablespoons fresh lemon juice
3 tablespoons olive oil, divided
1 (5-pound) whole chicken
2 lemons, thinly sliced
1 celery rib, cut into thirds
1 carrot, cut into thirds
1 small onion, halved
Vegetable cooking spray
1¼ teaspoons salt, divided
½ teaspoon pepper, divided
2 pounds small new potatoes, halved
¾ teaspoon dried rosemary
2 cups chicken broth
Fresh spinach leaves (optional)

WHISK together Greek seasoning, lemon juice, and 2 tablespoons olive oil in a small bowl.

LOOSEN skin from chicken breasts and drumsticks without detaching skin. Rub Greek seasoning mixture evenly under skin. Arrange 3 lemon slices on each side of breast under skin; carefully replace skin. Place remaining lemon slices and next 3 ingredients into chicken cavity. Tie ends of legs together with string; tuck wingtips under.

PLACE chicken, breast side up, on a lightly greased rack in a lightly greased shallow roasting pan. Lightly coat chicken with cooking spray; sprinkle evenly with 1 teaspoon salt and ¼ teaspoon pepper.

BAKE at 450° for 30 minutes.

STIR together potatoes, rosemary, and remaining each

Romaine Salad With Raspberry Salad Dressing

of 1 tablespoon oil, ¼ teaspoon salt, and ¼ teaspoon pepper in a bowl.

REMOVE chicken from oven; reduce oven temperature to 400°. Pour chicken broth over chicken. Arrange potato mixture in a single layer on rack around chicken; return to oven.

BAKE at 400° for 45 minutes or until a meat thermometer inserted into thigh registers 180°, basting every 15 minutes with pan juices. Cover loosely with aluminum foil to prevent excessive browning, if necessary. Remove from oven, and let stand 10 minutes before carving. Serve chicken and potatoes over fresh spinach leaves drizzled with pan juices, if desired. (The hot pan juices will wilt the spinach.)

Sautéed Zucchini and Yellow Squash

MAKES 6 SERVINGS
PREP: 10 MIN., COOK: 6 MIN.

3 small zucchini, sliced
3 yellow squash, sliced
2 tablespoons olive oil
1 garlic clove, minced
½ teaspoon salt
½ teaspoon freshly ground pepper

SAUTÉ zucchini and squash in hot olive oil in a skillet over medium-high heat 5 minutes or until crisp-tender. Stir in garlic and remaining ingredients; cook, stirring constantly, 1 minute. Serve immediately.

Slices of lemon are tucked under the skin and an herb mixture is rubbed under the skin of this Greek Roasted Chicken served on a bed of spinach with Rosemary Potatoes.

Cook's Notes

Associate Foods Editor Mary Allen Perry shared some thoughts for preparing a fabulous Greek Roasted Chicken:

■ Selecting a chicken: Choose the full-breasted, tender whole chicken usually labeled "roaster"; average weight is 5 to 6 pounds. It has more meat and often is more juicy. Whole, young broiler-fryers are equally as good to roast; however, the smaller weight (3 to 4½ pounds) will serve only 3 to 4.

■ Place the seasoning blend, lemon juice, and olive oil mixture under the skin, next to the meat you want to flavor.

■ Storing dried herbs: Don't store in the freezer; freezing doesn't extend the shelf life, and condensation will form in bottles during the time they are out of the freezer, quickening deterioration. Instead, close bottle tightly and avoid storing over a stove, sink, dishwasher, or above under-counter lighting.

■ Roasting poultry: Start with a hot, 450° oven to brown the outside of the bird and lock in juices. Reduce temperature to 400° after 30 minutes. Invest in a meat thermometer to check doneness.

■ Standing time: Just 10 minutes locks in the juices in the chicken. If cut too soon, juices run out onto the platter.

Banana-Chocolate Chip Cupcakes With Peanut Butter-Fudge Frosting

Banana-Chocolate Chip Cupcakes With Peanut Butter-Fudge Frosting

MAKES 2½ DOZEN
PREP: 30 MIN., BAKE: 25 MIN.

⅔ cup butter or margarine, softened
2 cups sugar
4 large eggs
3 large ripe bananas, mashed
1 cup buttermilk
1 teaspoon baking soda

3 cups all-purpose flour
2 teaspoons baking powder
¾ cup semisweet chocolate mini-morsels
Peanut Butter-Fudge Frosting
Dried banana chips (optional)

BEAT butter at medium speed with an electric mixer until creamy. Gradually add sugar, beating well. Add eggs, 1 at a time, beating well after each addition. Add bananas, beating just until blended.

STIR together buttermilk and baking soda. Combine flour and baking powder; gradually add to butter mixture alternately with buttermilk mixture, beginning and ending with flour mixture. Beat at low speed until blended after each addition. Stir in morsels. Spoon batter into 30 paper-lined cups in muffin pans, filling each three-fourths full.

BAKE at 350° for 20 to 25 minutes or until a wooden

Bring Out Your Best

Don't keep your best china in the closet just because the party is casual. It lends a touch of unexpected elegance to casual pottery, cotton napkins, and basic glassware. Keys to success: A unifying color (green) and the scalloped edge of the pottery plate is dressier and therefore more compatible to china than a plain edge. Sheet moss, glued to a cake round with spray adhesive, makes a clever charger plate to frame the plates.

pick inserted in center comes out clean. Remove cupcakes from pan, and cool on wire racks. Spread Peanut Butter-Fudge Frosting evenly over tops of cupcakes. Top with banana chips, if desired.

Peanut Butter-Fudge Frosting:

MAKES ABOUT 3½ CUPS
PREP: 10 MIN.

1⅔ cups peanut butter and milk chocolate morsels
½ cup butter or margarine, softened

1 (16-ounce) package powdered sugar
⅓ cup milk

MELT morsels according to package directions.
BEAT butter at medium speed with an electric mixer until creamy; gradually add powdered sugar, alternately with milk, beating until light and creamy. Gradually add melted morsels, beating just until blended.

Lemon Tartlets

MAKES 6 SERVINGS
PREP: 30 MIN., COOK: 5 MIN., CHILL: 8 HRS.,
BAKE: 10 MIN., COOL: 15 MIN.

Phyllo pastry sheets are found in the frozen dessert aisle of the grocery store. We find the sheets separate best when the package is thawed overnight in the refrigerator.

2 cups water
¼ cup cornstarch
¼ cup fresh lemon juice
½ cup no-calorie sweetener
¼ cup egg substitute

1 tablespoon grated lemon rind
12 frozen phyllo pastry sheets, thawed
Butter-flavored cooking spray
6 fresh whole strawberries

BRING first 3 ingredients to a boil in a large saucepan over medium-high heat, whisking constantly. Remove pan from heat.
WHISK together no-calorie sweetener, egg substitute, and lemon rind in a large bowl. Gradually pour hot lemon juice mixture into egg substitute mixture, whisking constantly. Cover bowl with plastic wrap, and chill 8 hours or until set.
STACK 2 phyllo sheets, spraying tops of each with cooking spray. (Keep remaining phyllo sheets covered with a damp towel.) Fold phyllo stack in half, connecting short sides. Fold phyllo in half again, connecting short sides. Fit into a cup of a muffin pan. Repeat procedure with remaining phyllo sheets.
BAKE at 375° for 10 minutes or until golden. Cool phyllo cups in pan on a wire rack 15 minutes or until completely cool. Remove phyllo cups from pan.
STIR chilled lemon mixture until smooth; spoon evenly into phyllo cups. Top each with a strawberry, and serve immediately.
NOTE: For testing purposes only, we used SPLENDA® Granular for no-calorie sweetener.

Clever Containers

Search flea markets, garage sales, or your attic for an eclectic mix of teapots or vases. Cari South, a *Southern Living* photo stylist, says, "Often a group of containers has more personality in the center of the table than one large mixed-flower arrangement. Decorate in odd numbers—three, five, or seven. Unify the grouping by filling each container with one or two varieties of complementing flowers, but in different colors. We used pink and peach snapdragons and purple hybrid delphinium."

How To Make the Teapot Arrangement:

Long-stemmed flowers placed in a relatively short container such as a teapot tend to be top-heavy and fall out of the pot unless secured. To solve, trim a block of water-soaked florist foam with a knife to a size that snuggly fits in the teapot opening. Insert flower stems, at slight angles, into foam to create a bouquet appearance. You can also place a florist's "frog" (a disc of upright metal prongs) in the teapot; fill the teapot with water. Gently push flower stems into prongs.

A garden party
Trimmed in White

Let the garden inspire a spring menu and a
refreshing mix of color.

Celebrations in a garden impart a sense of romance and enchantment. Whether you're planning an intimate dinner party or a charming wedding party, consider soft whites and ivories as an elegant backdrop to your outdoor tablescape.

Let the season dictate your color scheme. Spring offers a soft palette that gives simple style to any menu. Subtle textures of white mixed with pale yellows and splashes of greenery make an eye-catching buffet of garden-inspired recipes. Add a touch of color with antique floral china.

The golden tones of Broiled Yellow Tomatoes and the vibrant greens of Steamed Asparagus and Green Beans bring a bouquet of colors to neutral white serving pieces and layered linens. Garnishes of lemons and fresh herbs with loose arrangements of white and yellow daisies complement the setting.

Whichever accents you choose, a background of white lends versatility to the menu, accessories, and finishing touches for your special affair.

An Enchanted Menu
Serves 24

Garden Salad

Chicken Tetrazzini

Broiled Yellow Tomatoes

Steamed Asparagus and Green Beans
With Fresh Lemon-Basil Dip

Lemon Muffins

Mocha Charlottes

Lemonade or Iced tea

(above) Mix and match heirloom crystal vases to display a casual gathering of garden flowers.
(left) A breezy day inspires an inviting seating area for guests.

Yellow squash slices in Garden Salad help carry out the party's color scheme.

Garden Salad

MAKES 24 SERVINGS
PREP: 20 MIN.

6 (5-ounce) packages gourmet mixed salad greens
1 large red onion, halved and thinly sliced
2 red bell peppers, cut into thin strips

4 small yellow squash, thinly sliced
Vinaigrette Salad Dressing

TOSS together first 4 ingredients, and serve with dressing.

Vinaigrette Salad Dressing:

MAKES 3 CUPS
PREP: 10 MIN.

1 cup apple cider vinegar
6 tablespoons chopped onion
5 tablespoons sugar
2 large garlic cloves

2 teaspoons salt
2 teaspoons dry mustard
1 teaspoon pepper
2 cups vegetable oil

PROCESS first 7 ingredients in a blender until smooth. With blender running, add oil in a slow, steady stream; process until smooth. Cover and chill until ready to serve.

Chicken Tetrazzini

MAKES 8 SERVINGS
PREP: 30 MIN., COOK: 12 MIN., BAKE: 35 MIN.

This scrumptious casserole can easily be made ahead. We prepared three to serve a party of 24.

12 ounces uncooked vermicelli
½ cup butter or margarine
½ medium-size sweet onion, diced
½ cup all-purpose flour
4 cups milk
½ cup dry white wine
2 tablespoons chicken bouillon granules

1 teaspoon seasoned pepper
1½ cups freshly grated Parmesan cheese, divided
4 cups diced cooked chicken
1 (6-ounce) jar sliced mushrooms, drained
1 cup soft breadcrumbs
2 tablespoons butter or margarine, melted

PREPARE pasta according to package directions; drain and set aside.

MELT ½ cup butter in a Dutch oven over medium-high heat; add diced onion, and sauté 5 minutes or until tender.

WHISK in flour until smooth, and cook, whisking constantly, 1 minute. Gradually add milk and wine; cook, whisking constantly, 5 to 6 minutes or until thickened.

ADD bouillon granules, seasoned pepper, and 1 cup cheese. Cook, whisking constantly, 1 minute or until bouillon granules dissolve and cheese melts. Remove from heat. Stir in chicken, pasta, and mushrooms. Spoon into a lightly greased 13- x 9-inch baking dish. (Cover and chill 8 hours or freeze up to 1 month, if desired; thaw overnight in refrigerator before baking.)

BAKE, covered, at 350° for 20 minutes. Stir together remaining ½ cup cheese, breadcrumbs, and 2 tablespoons melted butter, and sprinkle evenly over casserole. Bake 10 to 15 more minutes.

NOTE: To save storage room while freezing, line the baking dish with heavy-duty aluminum foil, leaving several inches of overhang around sides. Spray foil with cooking spray, and spoon mixture into foil-lined dish. Fold overhanging foil to cover casserole. Freeze until firm. Remove foil-lined casserole from baking dish, and store in a zip-top plastic freezer bag. Freeze up to 1 month. When ready to serve, remove foil, and place frozen casserole in original baking dish. Thaw in refrigerator, and bake as directed.

The bounty of spring's fresh produce takes center stage in this menu. A simple table setting highlights the rich colors of each dish.

Broiled Yellow Tomatoes

MAKES 24 SERVINGS
PREP: 15 MIN., COOK: 5 MIN.

*If you don't want to broil the tomatoes,
just slice and season as directed.*

12 large yellow or red
tomatoes, cut in half
¼ cup olive oil
Salt and seasoned pepper to
taste

½ cup chopped fresh chives
24 small fresh dill sprigs

BRUSH cut sides of tomatoes with olive oil, and sprinkle with a pinch of salt and seasoned pepper.
BROIL 6 inches from heat 5 minutes or until thoroughly heated. Sprinkle evenly with chives; top each with a fresh dill sprig.

Steamed Asparagus and Green Beans With Fresh Lemon-Basil Dip

MAKES ABOUT 24 SERVINGS
PREP: 20 MIN., COOK: 8 MIN.

1 cup chopped fresh basil
2 cups mayonnaise
1 (8-ounce) container sour
cream
2 tablespoons grated lemon
rind

¼ teaspoon salt
4 pounds fresh asparagus
2 pounds fresh green beans,
trimmed
Garnishes: fresh basil leaves,
lemon curls and slices

WHISK together first 5 ingredients until blended. Cover and chill until ready to serve.
SNAP off tough ends of asparagus. Cook in boiling water to cover 2 to 3 minutes or until crisp-tender; drain. Plunge into ice water to stop the cooking process; drain.
COOK beans in boiling water to cover 3 to 5 minutes or until crisp-tender. Plunge into ice water to stop the cooking process; drain.
COVER and chill vegetables until ready to serve with dip. Garnish dip with fresh basil leaves, if desired. Garnish vegetables with lemon curls and slices, if desired.

Lemon Muffins

MAKES 2½ DOZEN
PREP: 20 MIN., BAKE: 12 MIN., COOL: 5 MIN.

1¾ cups all-purpose flour
1 teaspoon baking powder
¾ teaspoon baking soda
¼ teaspoon salt
1 tablespoon grated lemon rind
¾ cup sugar
1 large egg, lightly beaten

1 (8-ounce) container lemon
yogurt
6 tablespoons butter or
margarine, melted
1 tablespoon fresh lemon juice
Glaze

COMBINE first 6 ingredients in a large bowl; make a well in center of mixture.
STIR together egg and next 3 ingredients until blended. Add to dry ingredients, stirring just until moistened. Spoon into lightly greased miniature muffin pans, filling three-fourths full.
BAKE at 400° for 10 to 12 minutes or until lightly browned. Cool in pans 5 minutes. Prepare Glaze.
SPOON warm Glaze evenly over warm muffins. Remove from pans, and cool completely.
NOTE: To make ahead, place unglazed baked muffins in zip-top freezer bags, and freeze up to 1 month. Thaw; reheat, if desired.

Glaze:

MAKES ⅓ CUP
PREP: 5 MIN., COOK: 5 MIN.

¼ cup sugar
2 teaspoons grated lemon rind

⅓ cup fresh lemon juice

COOK all ingredients in a small saucepan over medium heat, stirring constantly, just until sugar dissolves.

Mocha Charlottes

MAKES 8 SERVINGS
PREP: 20 MIN., STAND: 9 MIN.,
COOK: 5 MIN., CHILL: 8 HRS.

*For a quick version of this dessert, line
teacups with ladyfingers, fill with chocolate
ice cream, and top with whipped cream.
Make three recipes to serve 24 guests.*

1 envelope unflavored gelatin
¼ cup cold water
½ cup granulated sugar
2 large eggs
1 cup milk
⅓ cup semisweet chocolate
morsels
1½ teaspoons instant coffee
granules

2 teaspoons vanilla extract
1½ cups whipping cream,
divided
2 (3-ounce) packages
ladyfingers, split crosswise
3 tablespoons powdered
sugar
Garnish: 8 (3-inch) cinnamon
sticks

SPRINKLE gelatin over ¼ cup cold water; stir and let stand 1 minute. Set gelatin mixture aside.
BEAT granulated sugar and eggs at medium speed with an electric mixer 2 to 3 minutes or until thick and pale.
HEAT milk in a large saucepan over low heat. Gradually add about one-fourth of hot milk to egg mixture; add to remaining hot milk, stirring constantly. Cook, stirring constantly, over low heat 4 to 5 minutes or until mixture coats a spoon. Remove from heat; stir in gelatin mixture until gelatin dissolves.
WHISK in chocolate morsels, coffee granules, and

Mocha Charlottes are served in dainty teacups with a dollop of sweetened whipped cream and a cinnamon stick.

vanilla until coffee granules dissolve and chocolate melts. Pour mixture into a large metal bowl; place bowl over ice, and let stand, stirring often, 6 to 8 minutes or until mixture is cold and slightly thickened.

BEAT 1 cup whipping cream at high speed until soft peaks form, and gradually fold into coffee mixture.

LINE 8 teacups with 6 ladyfinger halves each, placing rounded sides of ladyfingers against cup edges. Spoon custard evenly into cups; cover and chill 8 hours.

BEAT remaining ½ cup whipping cream and powdered sugar until soft peaks form. Top custards with whipped cream; garnish, if desired.

Loosely arranged mock orange and daisies help gather sheer fabric draped over chairs.

Name cards attached to organza bags filled with lemon mints hint of good things to come.

Wrap deli sandwiches in parchment paper, and tie with satin string. Tuck a daisy in the string for the finishing touch.

The Party Starts
in the Kitchen

Fresh ingredients and straightforward recipes keep this party focused on friends and the rewards of breaking bread together.

On a dazzling day, restaurateur and chef Frank Stitt and his wife, Pardis, are busy in their home kitchen preparing a meal for friends. The Stitts, proprietors of three Birmingham, Alabama, fine-dining eateries, prefer to keep gatherings intimate with 8 to 12 guests. Frank also prefers simple menus prepared from the very finest ingredients. "Pardis, my wife, and I love having salad with beautiful greens and an incredible vinaigrette made from special vinegar and olive oil. Even if the meal is just roast beef with horseradish and fried potatoes, it can be really great. You don't have to have a ton of different things for it to be a wonderful meal," says Frank.

Clearly, entertaining offers Frank a great deal more than just the enjoyment of good food and wine. "It's very spiritual to me to be at the table with friends," he muses. "I love to say grace. To break bread and share food is kind of like a sacrament to me." Join Frank in making your next meal special. Select one or all of the dishes here for your next event. You don't have to be a chef to make these recipes work.

Tapenade

MAKES 1 CUP
PREP: 10 MIN.

*Serve with fresh raw vegetables and
toasted French baguette slices.*

1 (6-ounce) jar pitted kalamata olives
(about 1½ cups)
1 small garlic clove
1 tablespoon drained capers
1 tablespoon sherry vinegar*
1 teaspoon lemon juice
¼ teaspoon freshly ground pepper
1 teaspoon rum (optional)
3 tablespoons extra-virgin olive oil

PULSE first 6 ingredients and, if
desired, rum in a blender or food
processor 3 or 4 times. Gradually
add oil; pulse 3 or 4 times or until
mixture forms a coarse paste, stopping to scrape down sides.
*White wine vinegar can be substi-
tuted for sherry vinegar.

Shrimp Tartlets

MAKES 2 DOZEN
PREP: 30 MIN., CHILL: 8 HRS., BAKE: 15 MIN.

*To streamline this recipe, we substituted
prepared phyllo pastry shells for home-
made cream puffs.*

2¼ cups water
¾ pound unpeeled, medium-size fresh
shrimp
½ cup grated Parmesan cheese, divided
1 (3-ounce) package cream cheese,
softened
¼ cup sour cream
1 green onion, minced
½ teaspoon Cajun seasoning
2 (2.1-ounce) packages frozen mini phyllo
pastry shells

BRING 2¼ cups water to a boil; add
shrimp, and cook 3 to 5 minutes or
just until shrimp turn pink. Drain
and rinse with cold water.
PEEL shrimp, and devein, if desired;
finely chop.
STIR together ¼ cup Parmesan cheese
and next 4 ingredients; stir in shrimp.
Cover and chill 8 hours.
BAKE pastry shells according to

package directions; cool completely.
Store in an airtight container 8
hours, if desired.
FILL baked pastry shells with shrimp
mixture. Place on baking sheets, and
sprinkle evenly with remaining ¼
cup Parmesan cheese.
BAKE at 325° for 10 to 15 minutes
or until thoroughly heated. Serve
immediately.
NOTE: To serve tartlets chilled, do
not bake after filling. Cover and chill
1 hour. Sprinkle with Parmesan
before serving.

(above) Pardis and Frank with a
bounty of fresh ingredients.
(left) The Stitts' spacious kitchen,
with its comfortable dining area,
provides plenty of room for food
and friends.

Double-Stuffed Eggs

MAKES 2 DOZEN
PREP: 30 MIN., CHILL: 8 HRS.

The potato flakes make a full-bodied filling, perfect for piping. One basic recipe makes three variations to chill overnight.

1 dozen hard-cooked eggs, peeled
¾ cup light mayonnaise
½ cup instant potato flakes
1 tablespoon Dijon mustard
¼ teaspoon salt
¼ teaspoon pepper
Garnish: fresh dill sprigs

CUT eggs in half lengthwise. Remove yolks, leaving egg whites intact. Process egg yolks, mayonnaise, and next 4 ingredients in a food processor until smooth, stopping to scrape down sides.

SPOON filling into egg whites. Cover and chill up to 8 hours. Garnish, if desired.

BACON-STUFFED EGGS: Stir ⅔ cup (8 slices) crumbled cooked bacon, 3 tablespoons pickle relish, and ¼ cup chopped fresh chives into egg mixture. Proceed as directed.

SHRIMP-STUFFED EGGS: Stir ¾ pound fresh shrimp, cooked, peeled, and chopped; 2 tablespoons prepared horseradish; and 6 green onions, minced, into egg mixture. Proceed as directed.

Lamb Chops With Mint Aïoli

MAKES 6 TO 8 SERVINGS
PREP: 15 MIN., BAKE: 40 MIN.

6 garlic cloves, minced
2 teaspoons dried summer savory
1 teaspoon salt
1 teaspoon pepper
16 (2-inch-thick) lamb chops
1 tablespoon olive oil
Mint Aïoli
Garnish: fresh mint sprigs

Lamb Chops With Mint Aïoli and New Potato Gratin With Lima Beans and Egg offer new and refreshing twists to this simple seasonal menu.

COMBINE first 4 ingredients; rub evenly onto both sides of lamb chops.

BROWN chops in hot oil in a large nonstick skillet over medium-high heat 2 to 3 minutes on each side. Arrange chops on a lightly greased rack in a broiler pan.

BAKE chops at 350° for 35 to 40 minutes or until a meat thermometer inserted into thickest portion registers 145° (medium rare). Serve lamb with Mint Aïoli. Garnish, if desired.

Mint Aïoli:

MAKES 1¼ CUPS
PREP: 5 MIN.

1 cup mayonnaise
¼ cup coarsely chopped fresh mint
4 garlic cloves, minced
1 teaspoon grated lemon rind
2 tablespoons fresh lemon juice
½ teaspoon salt
½ teaspoon pepper

PROCESS all ingredients in a blender or food processor until smooth, stopping to scrape down sides.

New Potato Gratin With Lima Beans and Egg

MAKES 6 TO 8 SERVINGS
PREP: 40 MIN., BAKE: 10 MIN.

6 small new potatoes, thinly sliced
½ cup frozen large lima beans, thawed
3 stale French bread slices
¼ cup (1 ounce) shredded Gruyère cheese
¼ cup (1 ounce) shredded Parmesan cheese
3 hard-cooked eggs, quartered
½ teaspoon salt
½ teaspoon pepper
½ cup whipping cream

COOK potato slices in boiling, salted water to cover 13 minutes. Add beans, and cook 2 more minutes. Remove from heat; drain well.

PULSE bread slices in a blender or food processor 8 to 10 times or until bread is crumbly.

PLACE potato slices and lima beans in a greased 10-inch deep-dish pieplate; sprinkle with half of Gruyère and half of Parmesan. Top evenly with egg; sprinkle with remaining cheeses, salt, and pepper. Pour whipping cream around inside edge of pieplate; sprinkle evenly with breadcrumbs.

BAKE at 475° for 10 minutes or until lightly browned.

Asparagus With Garlic Cream

MAKES 8 TO 10 SERVINGS
PREP: 20 MIN., COOK: 3 MIN., CHILL: 8 HRS.

1 (8-ounce) container sour cream
2 tablespoons milk
1 tablespoon white wine vinegar
1 tablespoon olive oil
¼ teaspoon salt
¼ teaspoon freshly ground pepper
2 garlic cloves, minced
2 pounds fresh asparagus

STIR together first 7 ingredients. Cover and chill 8 hours.

SNAP off tough ends of asparagus. Cook in boiling water to cover 3 minutes or until crisp-tender; drain.

PLUNGE asparagus into ice water to stop the cooking process; drain.

SERVE with garlic cream.

A layer of pastry cream snuggles beneath a blanket of fresh berries in this Strawberry Tart, a classic French dessert.

Strawberry Tart

MAKES 8 SERVINGS
PREP: 20 MIN., CHILL: 5 HRS., BAKE: 18 MIN.

1½ cups all-purpose flour
½ teaspoon salt
⅓ cup sugar
⅓ cup cold butter or margarine, cut up
2 tablespoons cold shortening
3 tablespoons cold water
½ cup sugar
¼ cup cornstarch
2 cups half-and-half
5 egg yolks
1 teaspoon rose water or orange-flower
    water (optional)
3 tablespoons butter or margarine
1 teaspoon vanilla extract
1 quart fresh strawberries, sliced
Garnish: fresh mint sprig

PULSE first 3 ingredients in a blender or food processor 3 or 4 times or until combined.

ADD ⅓ cup butter and 2 tablespoons shortening; pulse 5 or 6 times or until crumbly. With blender or processor running, gradually add 3 tablespoons water, and process until dough forms a ball and leaves sides of bowl, adding more water if necessary. Wrap dough in plastic wrap, and chill 1 hour.

ROLL dough to ⅛-inch thickness on a lightly floured surface. Press onto bottom and up sides of a 9-inch tart pan. Line dough with parchment paper; fill with pie weights or dried beans.

BAKE at 425° for 15 minutes. Remove weights and parchment paper, and bake 3 more minutes.

COMBINE ½ cup sugar and ¼ cup cornstarch in a medium saucepan.

WHISK together half-and-half, egg yolks, and, if desired, rose water. Gradually whisk half-and-half mixture into sugar mixture in saucepan over medium heat. Bring to a boil, and cook, whisking constantly, 1 minute. Remove from heat.

STIR in 3 tablespoons butter and 1 teaspoon vanilla; cover and chill at least 4 hours. Spoon into prepared pastry shell; top with strawberry slices, and garnish, if desired. Serve immediately.

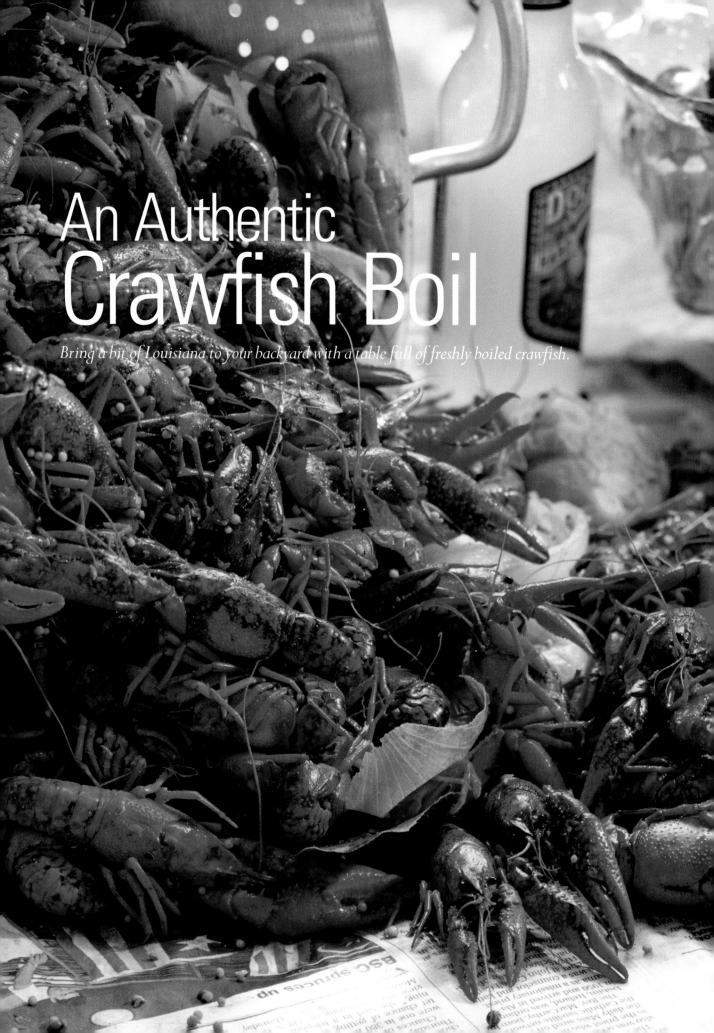

An Authentic
Crawfish Boil

Bring a bit of Louisiana to your backyard with a table full of freshly boiled crawfish.

The crawfish boil is a culinary and social rite of spring in Louisiana. This customary gathering gives a warm welcome to sunshine and an official goodbye to all things wintry and gray.

If you're unfamiliar with this tasty tradition, we've asked Andrew Jaeger, owner of Andrew Jaeger's House of Seafood in New Orleans, to reveal the finer points of cooking up these tiny freshwater crustaceans. His father, Charles Jaeger, was one of the first businessmen to bring live crawfish into New Orleans on a large scale. Andrew also shares his family's secret Crawfish Boil recipe.

"Each person has his or her own special way of doing things, but there are really two important rules to remember when boiling crawfish. First, you want to use only live crawfish, so throw out those that don't move. Second, as far as the actual cooking goes, it's really a little boil and a lot of soak," says Andrew. Over-boiling crawfish makes them mushy, which is why the soaking stage is so critical. He continues, "This allows the seasonings to gently seep into the shells; so the longer you allow them to soak, the more flavorful and spicy they become. Just taste them along the way to make sure they don't overcook."

Crawfish season gets rolling about April and ends around June. But if you just can't do without the taste of crawfish in the off-season, many grocery stores and fish markets sell tail meat cooked, peeled, and frozen, perfect for recipes such as crawfish étouffée. Andrew says, "It's really not a bad product. It's easy to use, and the meat is packed in its own delicious fat. However, fat is important for flavor, so don't wash it off."

Crawfish To Go

If live crawfish aren't available at your local grocery or fish market, try these sources.
- Louisiana Cajun Crawfish — (504) 231-1067 or visit www.crawfishguy.com.
- Louisiana Crawfish Company — (888) 522-7292 or visit www.lacrawfish.com.

Crawfish, which hail from Louisiana's Atchafalaya Basin, are boiled up by the ton at large festivals in towns such as Pierre Part and Breaux Bridge.

Crawfish Boil

MAKES 5 POUNDS
PREP: 1 HR., COOK: 55 MIN., STAND: 30 MIN.

1½ gallons water	1 tablespoon black peppercorns
10 bay leaves	1 teaspoon whole cloves
1 cup salt	4 celery ribs, quartered
¾ cup ground red pepper	3 medium onions, halved
¼ cup whole allspice	3 garlic bulbs, halved
2 tablespoons mustard seeds	crosswise
1 tablespoon coriander seeds	5 pounds whole crawfish
1 tablespoon dill seeds	
1 tablespoon dried crushed red pepper	

BRING 1½ gallons water to a boil in a 19-quart stockpot over high heat. Add bay leaves and next 12 ingredients to water. Return to a rolling boil. Reduce heat to medium, and cook, uncovered, 30 minutes.

ADD crawfish. Bring to a rolling boil over high heat; cook 5 minutes.

REMOVE stockpot from heat; let stand 30 minutes. (For spicier crawfish, let stand 45 minutes.)

DRAIN crawfish. Serve on large platters or newspaper.

Crawfish Eatin' 101

For those unfamiliar with the "art" of eating crawfish, here's a quick primer on dealing with these delicious crustaceans.
- Begin by snapping apart the head and the tail.
- If you're not a fan of the head, toss it aside, then peel the tail by working your thumbs down the sides of the hard shell, releasing the sweet meat.
- For the true crawfish lover, the renowned "sucking of the head" gives full access to a fiery concoction of spices from the cooking liquid and fat from the crawfish—a treat not to be missed by true aficionados.

Great Flavors for Passover

Serve fall-off-the-bone Braised Short Ribs or Saucy Brisket and tender veggies with tasty trimmings for a homestyle dinner.

Many Jewish families delight in special recipes during the annual Seder, the feast commemorating the exodus of the Israelites from Egypt, celebrated on the first or first and second evenings of Passover. Some look forward to slow-cooked brisket, while others anticipate roasted lamb or crispy fried fish as the main dish.

If you don't celebrate Passover, you'll still want to satisfy your family's craving for a hearty, full-flavored meal. Tender and juicy meat dishes, not-the-least-bit-greasy fried fritters, and other simple recipes make great picks for any night. *Joy E. Zacharia*

Date-Orange-Nut Spread

MAKES 2 CUPS
PREP: 20 MIN., CHILL: 8 HRS.

This sweet spread made of fruits and nuts is often served with matzo (crisp unleavened bread). It's also a delicious accompaniment with beef and lamb.

1½ cups chopped dates
½ cup raisins
½ cup sweet white wine
½ teaspoon grated orange rind
1 large navel orange, peeled and cut into chunks
⅓ cup honey
½ cup almonds, toasted
½ cup walnuts, toasted
½ teaspoon ground cinnamon
¼ teaspoon ground cardamom

COMBINE dates and raisins in a bowl; add wine. Cover and chill 8 hours.

PROCESS date mixture, orange rind, and remaining ingredients in a food processor until slightly chunky and spreadable, adding more wine if needed.

NOTE: For testing purposes only, we used Sunsweet chopped dates and Mogen David white wine.

Spinach Salad With Apricot Vinaigrette

MAKES 6 SERVINGS
PREP: 10 MIN.

2 (6-ounce) packages fresh baby spinach
1 pint grape tomatoes, halved
1 small red onion, thinly sliced
½ cup chopped dried apricots
1 ripe avocado, peeled and diced
½ cup chopped pecans, toasted
Apricot Vinaigrette

PLACE first 6 ingredients in a large bowl, tossing gently. Drizzle with Apricot Vinaigrette, tossing gently to coat.

Apricot Vinaigrette:

MAKES ½ CUP
PREP: 5 MIN.

⅓ cup vegetable oil
2 tablespoons white wine vinegar
2 tablespoons orange juice
2 tablespoons apricot jam
½ teaspoon salt
½ teaspoon ground coriander
½ teaspoon freshly ground pepper

WHISK together all ingredients in a small bowl.

Braised Short Ribs (page 27) take some time to cook, but after one hearty bite, you'll agree they're worth every second.

Light and colorful Spinach Salad With Apricot Vinaigrette (page 24) is sweet, sour, and full of veggies. To serve salad for dinner, top with grilled chicken or tuna.

Chicken Soup With Matzo Balls

MAKES 6 QUARTS
PREP: 35 MIN., COOK: 1 HR.

8 carrots
2 parsnips
5 celery ribs
3 sweet onions
1 (2½- to 3-pound) whole chicken
10 cups water
8 chicken bouillon cubes
Matzo Balls

CUT first 3 ingredients into 2-inch pieces; cut onions in half. Place vegetables, chicken, water, and bouillon cubes in a Dutch oven; bring to a boil. Reduce heat, and simmer, covered, 1 hour or until chicken is tender. Remove chicken and vegetables from broth with a slotted spoon; cool slightly. Bone chicken, and cut into bite-size pieces; set aside. Process vegetables in a food processor until smooth.
SKIM fat from broth. Stir vegetable puree and chicken into broth. Cook over medium heat, stirring occasionally, until thoroughly heated. Serve with Matzo Balls.

Matzo Balls:

MAKES 1 DOZEN
PREP: 15 MIN., CHILL: 30 MIN., COOK: 30 MIN.

4 large eggs, lightly beaten
1½ cups matzo ball mix*
¼ cup canola oil
½ teaspoon salt
6 cups water

STIR together first 4 ingredients; cover and chill 30 minutes. Shape mixture into 1-inch balls. (Do not exceed this size.)
BRING 6 cups water to a boil in a medium saucepan; drop balls into boiling water. Cover and simmer 30 minutes. Remove from water with a slotted spoon.
*During Passover use kosher matzo ball mix.

Soothing Chicken Soup With Matzo Balls gets its color and earthy flavor from carrots, parsnips, and celery.

Saucy Brisket

MAKES 8 SERVINGS
PREP: 10 MIN., BAKE: 3 HRS.

For a healthier version, prepare this a day or two ahead. Just before reheating, skim off the fat and place the brisket in a low oven (250° to 300°) until heated through.

1 (4- to 5-pound) beef brisket
2 tablespoons vegetable oil
1 (8-ounce) package sliced fresh mushrooms
½ cup firmly packed brown sugar
½ cup barbecue sauce
½ cup ketchup
½ cup cider vinegar
½ cup duck sauce
1 (1-ounce) envelope dry onion soup mix
1 cup water
4 bay leaves
4 large baking potatoes, each cut into 8 wedges (optional)

BROWN brisket on both sides in hot oil in a Dutch oven over medium-high heat, and place in a large roasting pan.
STIR together mushrooms and next 6 ingredients; spread over brisket.
BAKE, covered, at 350° for 1 hour. Add 1 cup water and bay leaves, and bake, covered, 1 hour and 30 minutes. Add potato, if desired, and bake, uncovered, 30 minutes or until potato is tender. Discard bay leaves.
CUT brisket diagonally across the grain into thin slices. Serve with sauce and, if desired, potato.
NOTE: Look for duck sauce in the Asian foods section of your local supermarket.

Braised Short Ribs

MAKES 6 SERVINGS
PREP: 35 MIN., CHILL: 6 HRS., BAKE: 3 HRS., COOK: 15 MIN.

Red wine gives this rich-tasting dish a smooth yet bold flavor.

2¼ cups dry red wine, divided
2¼ cups beef broth, divided
2 garlic cloves, chopped
1 teaspoon ground allspice
½ teaspoon ground ginger
4 pounds beef short ribs, trimmed
1 teaspoon salt
1 teaspoon pepper
3 tablespoons olive oil
1 carrot, chopped
½ onion, chopped
1 celery rib, chopped
2 tablespoons tomato paste
Garnish: chopped fresh parsley

COMBINE ¼ cup wine, ¼ cup broth, garlic, allspice, and ginger in a large shallow dish; add ribs, turning to coat. Cover and chill 4 to 6 hours, turning occasionally.
REMOVE ribs from marinade, reserving marinade. Sprinkle ribs with salt and pepper.
COOK ribs, in batches, in hot oil in a Dutch oven over medium-high heat 15 minutes or until browned. Remove ribs, and set aside.
REDUCE heat to medium; add carrot, onion, and celery, and sauté 7 minutes or until browned. Add tomato paste; cook, stirring constantly, 3 minutes.
RETURN ribs to Dutch oven. Stir in reserved marinade and remaining 2 cups each of wine and broth; bring to a boil, and tightly cover.
BAKE at 300° for 3 hours. Remove ribs.
SKIM fat from sauce, and simmer sauce 12 to 15 minutes or until reduced by half. Serve sauce with ribs. Garnish, if desired.

Passover Primer

Widely followed dietary restrictions include:

■ No wheat flour or leavening agents (baking powder or soda, yeast): During the ancient deliverance, Jews did not have time to wait for bread to rise.
■ Ordinary grains: Only "Kosher for Passover"-labeled matzo can be used.
■ Legumes (peas, beans, lentils)
■ Kosher wine: Think the only kosher wine is as sweet and purple as grape juice? Think again. Great-tasting wines at various prices await you at www.kosherwine.com.

For related information on the holiday, visit www.holidays.net/passover.

Matzo is a flat, crisp bread baked without any leavening. It's traditionally eaten during Passover.

For a unique side dish, try perfectly fried
Leek-and-Potato Fritters. Serve them alongside
eggs for brunch, too.

Leek-and-Potato Fritters

MAKES 18 PATTIES
PREP: 30 MIN., CHILL: 1 HR., COOK: 4 MIN. PER BATCH

According to kosher dietary laws, if the main dish is meat or poultry, serve fritters with applesauce. If fish or a meatless dish is the entrée, serve with sour cream and/or applesauce.

1 large russet potato, peeled and cut into
  2-inch pieces (about ½ pound)
1 teaspoon salt
2 pounds leeks, thinly sliced
4 large eggs, lightly beaten
½ cup matzo meal or fine, dry breadcrumbs*
⅓ cup grated Parmesan cheese
1 teaspoon salt
¾ teaspoon freshly ground pepper
½ cup canola oil
Sour cream (optional)

COOK potato and 1 teaspoon salt in a Dutch oven in boiling water to cover 20 minutes or until tender; drain. Mash potato, and set aside.
COOK leeks in Dutch oven in boiling water to cover 3 minutes; drain.
STIR together potato, leeks, and next 5 ingredients. Chill 1 hour. Shape mixture into 18 patties.
COOK in batches in hot oil in a large skillet 2 minutes on each side or until golden brown. Serve immediately with sour cream, if desired.
*During Passover use kosher matzo meal.

Mushroom Matzo Kugel

MAKES 6 SERVINGS
PREP: 20 MIN., BAKE: 30 MIN.

Double this stuffinglike recipe, and freeze half before baking, if desired.

1 small onion, diced
3 celery ribs, diced
1 (8-ounce) package sliced fresh
  mushrooms
⅓ cup canola oil
3½ cups matzo farfel
2 large eggs, lightly beaten
1 (10½-ounce) can chicken broth, undiluted
1¼ cups hot water
1 teaspoon salt
¼ teaspoon pepper

SAUTÉ first 3 ingredients in hot oil in a large skillet until tender; remove from heat.
STIR in matzo farfel and remaining ingredients. Spoon into a lightly greased 1½-quart baking dish.
BAKE at 375° for 30 minutes.

Soft Coconut Macaroons

MAKES 2 DOZEN
PREP: 10 MIN., BAKE: 20 MIN.

If you're not preparing macaroons for Passover, use ¼ cup all-purpose flour instead of ¼ cup matzo meal.

4 egg whites
2⅔ cups sweetened flaked coconut
⅔ cup sugar
¼ cup matzo meal
½ teaspoon clear vanilla extract*
¼ teaspoon salt
¼ to ½ teaspoon almond extract

Moist, chewy, and very traditional, Soft Coconut Macaroons are a sweet treat at the end of any meal.

STIR together all ingredients in a large bowl, blending well. Drop by teaspoonfuls onto lightly greased baking sheets.
BAKE at 325° for 18 to 20 minutes. Remove to wire racks to cool.
*Using clear vanilla extract will keep the macaroons pearly white, but if you don't have it, use regular vanilla.

Choose challah bread for Make-Ahead French Toast With Strawberry Sauce.

Spinach-and-Bacon Quiche

MAKES 8 SERVINGS
PREP: 20 MIN., BAKE: 45 MIN.

1 (10-ounce) package frozen chopped spinach, thawed
4 large eggs, lightly beaten
1½ cups half-and-half
1 (1.8-ounce) package leek soup mix
¼ teaspoon pepper
10 bacon slices, cooked and crumbled
½ cup (2 ounces) shredded sharp Cheddar cheese
½ cup (2 ounces) shredded mozzarella cheese
1 unbaked (9-inch) frozen deep-dish pastry shell*

DRAIN thawed spinach well, pressing between layers of paper towels.
WHISK together eggs and next 3 ingredients. Stir in spinach, bacon, and cheeses. Pour mixture into frozen pastry shell; place on a baking sheet.
BAKE at 375° for 40 to 45 minutes.
*Substitute ½ (15-ounce) package refrigerated piecrusts. Prepare according to package directions.

Chicken and Grits

MAKES 4 TO 6 SERVINGS
PREP: 10 MIN., COOK: 15 MIN., BAKE: 30 MIN.

2 (14-ounce) cans chicken broth
1 cup uncooked quick-cooking grits
1 (8-ounce) jar process cheese spread
3 large eggs, lightly beaten
2 cups chopped cooked chicken
½ teaspoon poultry seasoning

BRING broth to a boil in a large saucepan over medium-high heat; stir in grits. Cover, reduce heat, and simmer 5 minutes; stir occasionally.
ADD cheese and remaining ingredients, stirring well. Pour into a greased 11- x 7- inch baking dish.
BAKE, uncovered, at 375° for 30 minutes.

Make-Ahead French Toast With Strawberry Sauce

MAKES 10 SERVINGS
PREP: 25 MIN., CHILL: 8 HRS., BAKE: 45 MIN.

Our Test Kitchens' staff found the light version of this recipe just as delicious as the original. Challah bread is a rich egg bread with a light, airy texture.

1 (16-ounce) challah bread loaf, cubed*
1 (8-ounce) package cream cheese, cut into pieces
6 large eggs
4 cups half-and-half
½ cup butter or margarine, melted
¼ cup maple syrup
2 cups fresh strawberries, sliced
1 (10-ounce) jar strawberry preserves

ARRANGE half of challah bread in a lightly greased 13- x 9-inch pan. Sprinkle with cheese pieces, and top with remaining bread.
WHISK together eggs and next 3 ingredients; pour over bread mixture, pressing bread cubes to absorb egg mixture. Cover and chill 8 hours.
BAKE, covered, at 350° for 25 minutes. Uncover and bake 20 more minutes.
HEAT sliced strawberries and strawberry preserves in a saucepan over low heat, and serve over toast.
*You can substitute French bread for challah.

TO LIGHTEN: Substitute 1 (8-ounce) package Neufchâtel cheese for cream cheese, 1½ cups egg substitute for eggs, and 4 cups fat-free half-and-half for half-and-half.

Gracious
Gathering

You can entertain in true Southern style—even with a busy schedule. Our do-ahead recipes make it easy.

Entertaining in grand style often gets lost in the wake of our fast-paced lives. Even in our hectic world, though, Southern style and hospitality still exist. The key is using modern conveniences to create a gracious setting and selecting a menu that works for you.

Our make-ahead menu fits right in with an atmosphere of tailored simplicity. Because all the recipes can be served chilled, you'll have plenty of time to spend with guests. Remember how easy your grandmother made it look? Now it's your turn. True elegance should appear natural and effortless—and with our help, it is.

The delicate flavor of chilled Cucumber Soup With Dill Cream is ideal for any afternoon setting.

Make-Ahead Menu
Serves 8

Miniature Tomato
Sandwiches

Cucumber Soup With Dill Cream

Crab Cakes With Sweet White
Corn-and-Tomato Relish

Marinated Green Bean-and-
Okra Salad

Rice Primavera Salad

Blueberry-Pecan Cobbler

Iced tea

Miniature Tomato Sandwiches

MAKES 16 APPETIZER SERVINGS
PREP: 10 MIN.

1 French baguette
¼ cup mayonnaise
1 (3-ounce) package cream cheese, softened
2 teaspoons chopped fresh basil
¼ teaspoon salt, divided
¼ teaspoon pepper, divided
4 plum tomatoes, sliced

CUT baguette into 16 slices.
STIR together mayonnaise, cream cheese, basil, ⅛ teaspoon salt, and ⅛ teaspoon pepper; cover and chill 8 hours, if desired.
SPREAD cheese mixture on 1 side of each baguette slice. Top evenly with tomatoes, and sprinkle with remaining salt and pepper.

Cucumber Soup With Dill Cream

MAKES 1½ QUARTS
PREP: 15 MIN., CHILL: 8 HRS.

2 cups half-and-half, divided
4 cucumbers, peeled, seeded, and chopped
2 green onions, sliced
1 tablespoon lemon juice
1 (16-ounce) container sour cream
½ teaspoon salt
½ teaspoon hot sauce
½ cup sour cream
1 tablespoon chopped fresh dill
Garnish: fresh dill sprig

PROCESS 1 cup half-and-half and next 3 ingredients in a blender or food processor until smooth, stopping to scrape down sides.
STIR together cucumber mixture, remaining 1 cup half-and-half, container of sour cream, salt, and hot sauce. Cover and chill 8 hours.
STIR together ½ cup sour cream and chopped dill; dollop on each serving. Garnish, if desired.

Crab Cakes With Sweet White
Corn-and-Tomato Relish

Crab Cakes With Sweet White Corn-and-Tomato Relish

MAKES 8 SERVINGS
PREP: 20 MIN., COOK: 8 MIN. PER BATCH

These crab cakes caught our attention with their colorful relish. Seasonal fresh corn and tomatoes make this accompaniment irresistible.

6 tablespoons butter, divided
1 small sweet onion, chopped
2 garlic cloves, minced
1 pound fresh lump crabmeat, drained
3 cups soft breadcrumbs, divided
¼ cup mayonnaise
1 large egg, lightly beaten
2 tablespoons chopped fresh parsley
1 tablespoon Dijon mustard
1 tablespoon Worcestershire sauce
¼ teaspoon salt
¼ teaspoon pepper
¼ teaspoon hot sauce
1 teaspoon lemon juice
Sweet White Corn-and-Tomato Relish

MELT 2 tablespoons butter in a large skillet over medium heat; add onion and garlic, and sauté until tender. Remove from heat; stir in crabmeat, 2 cups bread-crumbs, and next 9 ingredi-ents. Shape mixture into 8 patties; dredge in remaining 1 cup breadcrumbs.

MELT 2 tablespoons butter in a large skillet over medium-high heat; cook 4 crab cakes 3 to 4 minutes on each side or until golden. Drain on paper towels. Repeat procedure with remaining 2 tablespoons butter and crab cakes. Serve immediately with Sweet White Corn-and-Tomato Relish, or cover and chill up to 4 hours.

Sweet White Corn-and-Tomato Relish:

MAKES 3 CUPS
PREP: 15 MIN., COOK: 1 MIN., CHILL: 3 HRS.

4 ears fresh sweet white corn
2 large tomatoes, peeled and chopped
3 green onions, sliced
2 tablespoons lemon juice
1 tablespoon olive oil
½ teaspoon salt
½ teaspoon pepper
¼ teaspoon garlic salt
⅛ teaspoon hot sauce

COOK corn in boiling water to cover 1 minute; drain and cool. Cut kernels from cobs.

STIR together corn, tomatoes, and remaining ingredi-ents; cover and chill 3 hours.

NOTE: For sweet white corn, we used Silver Queen.

A single gardenia or magnolia blossom in a clear vase brings simplicity and style to the table.

Marinated Green Bean-and-Okra Salad

MAKES 8 SERVINGS
PREP: 15 MIN., COOK: 3 MIN., CHILL: 3 HRS.

1½ pounds fresh green beans, trimmed
1½ pounds small fresh okra
¾ cup olive oil
6 tablespoons white wine vinegar
1 tablespoon chopped fresh basil
½ teaspoon salt
½ teaspoon pepper
¼ teaspoon dry mustard
¼ cup crumbled feta cheese

COOK beans and okra in boiling water to cover 3 min-utes. Plunge beans and okra into ice water to stop the cooking process; drain.

WHISK together olive oil and next 5 ingredients; pour over beans and okra. Cover and chill 3 hours. Drain beans and okra; sprinkle with cheese before serving.

Table To Go

Dining outdoors is easy—especially with this table that can be assembled on the spot. For this story, we created an intimate dining area in the yard by using a 7-foot-long folding table and detachable plywood rectangles for the top.

Folding tables (available in 6- and 7-foot lengths) are found at home-center stores. Typically less than $50 each, these tables also are ideal for the overflow company during the holidays and other special occasions.

We enlarged our top surface to comfortably accommodate eight by placing three (40- x 30-inch) plywood rectangles over the top of the table to form one extended (40- x 90-inch) top. Using three sections instead of one makes the top more convenient to transport and store. Latch hooks and eye screws were installed underneath each corner to lock the pieces together when placed side by side. Small wooden pegs and adjacent holes were added along the edge for a tight fit.

When the party is over, unscrew the plywood, stack up the pieces, and fold up the table. The parts can be stored easily under a bed, in a closet, or in a garage.

The finishing touch is a tailored cloth custom-made to fit the tabletop's dimensions and hang to the ground. Made from sturdy cotton fabric, the cloth's corner pleats are simple details that give a crisp, summery look to the setting.

Rice Primavera Salad

MAKES 8 CUPS
PREP: 15 MIN., CHILL: 8 HRS.

2 zucchini	¾ cup mayonnaise
2 yellow squash	⅓ cup buttermilk
1 large red bell pepper, chopped	2 tablespoons Dijon mustard
1 medium-size red onion, chopped	2 tablespoons white vinegar
5 cups cooked long-grain rice	1½ teaspoons salt
	½ teaspoon pepper

CUT zucchini and yellow squash in half lengthwise; cut into slices.

STIR together vegetables, rice, and remaining ingredients; cover and chill 8 hours.

Blueberry-Pecan Cobbler

MAKES 4 SERVINGS
PREP: 15 MIN., BAKE: 20 MIN.

Double the recipe to serve eight guests.

4 pints fresh or frozen blueberries	1 teaspoon vanilla extract
1½ cups sugar	1 (15-ounce) package refrigerated piecrusts
½ cup all-purpose flour	½ cup chopped pecans, toasted
⅓ cup water	Vanilla ice cream (optional)
2 tablespoons lemon juice	Garnish: fresh mint sprigs
½ teaspoon ground cinnamon	

BRING first 7 ingredients to a boil in a saucepan over medium heat, stirring until sugar dissolves. Reduce heat to low; cook, stirring occasionally, 10 minutes.

SPOON half of blueberry mixture into a lightly greased 8-inch square pan. Roll 1 piecrust to ⅛-inch thickness on a lightly floured surface; cut into an 8-inch square. Place over blueberry mixture; sprinkle with pecans.

BAKE at 475° for 10 minutes. Spoon remaining blueberry mixture over baked crust.

ROLL remaining piecrust to ⅛-inch thickness; cut into 1-inch strips. Arrange in a lattice design over blueberry mixture.

BAKE at 475° for 10 minutes or until golden. Serve with vanilla ice cream, if desired; garnish, if desired.

Each bite of Blueberry-Pecan Cobbler contains two layers of crust and plenty of plump berries. We love it with or without ice cream.

Ice It Down

Try these cool ideas for entertaining.

Serve chilled wine and other cold
refreshments in style by using easy-to-make
ice bottle coolers.

Chilling enough drinks at a gathering can be a challenge, especially if you're short on refrigerator space. Try these creative and practical ideas the next time you have guests.

Choose watertight containers from items around your home, toolshed, or garden that are large enough to hold ice and drinks. If the perfect container isn't watertight, don't sweat it. You can line it across the bottom and up the sides with layers of heavy-duty aluminum foil or large plastic bags, then fill with ice. Hide edges of the foil or plastic lining by folding down and tucking them in. Add your beverages, then give them a few turns in the ice, and you're set. To quick-cool beverages, add a little salt to the ice. Just be sure not to pour out the salty leftovers in the yard because it might damage grass or plants.

Protect surfaces that could be damaged from the condensation by placing heavy plastic, covered with a large towel, under containers, or use a suitable tray. Two bowls, with one slightly larger than the other, nestled together also will work.

Vicki A. Poellnitz

Cool Around the House

- It's best to position the bar or beverage station out of the main traffic flow to avoid creating a bottleneck.
- Group baskets of various sizes together with a different type of drink in each one. Line baskets with plastic to avoid leaks.
- Grab your old footlocker from summer camp (as long as the hinges will hold the top open); line it with plastic, and fill to the brim with ice and beverages.
- For really large gatherings, consider chilling beverages in the bath tub.
- Dress up your beverage station with vases of greenery or flowers, ribbons, and candles.
- Tuck fresh flowers into the ice along with bottles or cans for a touch of color.
- Place a basket of insulated drink holders beside the beverages.
- Don't forget a stable work surface with a small cutting board and a paring knife for slicing limes or lemons. Include a corkscrew and bottle opener, a hand towel, and a lined trash can for empties and bottle caps.

Creative Coolers:
These frozen coolers will last 2 to 3 hours.

What you'll need:
- To make bottle coolers, use an empty, clear 3-liter plastic soft drink bottle or other large, wide plastic container.
- Save an empty 750-milliliter wine bottle from another event. Rinse it out, and air-dry.
- You'll also need: plastic wrap, a funnel, scissors, wooden skewers, florist tape, and distilled water. (Distilled water prevents cloudiness in ice.)
- Gather fresh flowers, small seashells, sliced citrus fruit, summer berries, fresh herbs, or other small items that complement your party's decor. They will need to fit between the plastic container and the empty wine bottle.

Here's how:
- Cut the plastic bottle or container 2 inches above the desired height of the finished frozen cooler.
- Wrap the empty wine bottle in plastic wrap.
- Place wrapped bottle in center of the plastic container.
- Secure tape to one side of plastic container. Continue up one side, over the top, and down other side of wine bottle, securing tape on opposite side of plastic container. Repeat procedure, forming an X across top of bottle. (This holds bottle in place when water is poured into plastic container.)

- Tightly fill the space between plastic container and wine bottle, in a decorative fashion, with selected objects. Use wooden skewers to push items snugly in the bottom curves of the plastic container and to readjust once water is added, if necessary.
- Using the funnel, fill with distilled water to 2 inches from the top of the plastic container.
- Freeze at least 24 hours.
- Remove from freezer, and let stand at room temperature 20 minutes. Remove tape, and hold bottle under cool running water to loosen plastic container. If you have trouble removing the plastic, cut the plastic bottle, beginning at the top edge, and continue cutting down side to remove.
- Fill wine bottle with hot water, and let stand 10 minutes, twisting bottle to dislodge. Discard wine bottle and plastic wrap. Place chilled bottle in frozen cooler to keep beverage cool before serving. Place bottle coolers on a tray or cloth napkin to catch drips.

An All-American
Picnic

Enjoy this picnic menu on the Capitol grounds

or in your own backyard.

On the Fourth of July, our nation celebrates in a big way. From backyard barbecues to the mega-gathering on The Mall in Washington, D.C., we come together to share our pride of place, patriotism, and love of a good party.

Wherever you plan to be, you'll need food. Use this menu to adorn your picnic blanket with a delicious but doable meal. Once you've claimed your spot, relax and raise a birthday toast. Take a nap on the grass, wave the flag, slice a watermelon. Then wait for the sun to slide below the trees so the fireworks spectacular can begin. It'll be a fitting end to a wonderfully festive day.

Independence Day Picnic
Serves 8

Roast Beef Wraps

Grilled Marinated Vegetable Salad

New Potato Salad

Creamy Dill Slaw

Granny Smith Apple Pie

Chocolate-Glazed Brownies

Watermelon

Lemonade and Assorted beverages

Roast Beef Wraps

MAKES 8 SERVINGS
PREP: 20 MIN., CHILL 8 HRS.

Mealtime's a wrap with these easy-to-prepare and easy-to-eat sandwiches.

½ cup sour cream*
½ cup mayonnaise*
1 green onion, chopped
2 tablespoons prepared horseradish
½ teaspoon salt
½ teaspoon pepper
8 (12-inch) flour tortillas
1 pound roast beef, cut into 24 thin slices
2 (6-ounce) packages deli-style sharp
  Cheddar cheese slices (optional)
2 cups shredded iceberg lettuce

STIR together first 6 ingredients until blended. Spread evenly on 1 side of each tortilla; top with 3 beef slices and, if desired, 2 cheese slices. Sprinkle each evenly with shredded lettuce.

ROLL up tortillas tightly; wrap in parchment paper or plastic wrap. Chill 8 hours.

NOTE: For testing purposes only, we used Sargento Deli Style Sharp Cheddar Cheese slices.

*Substitute ½ cup light sour cream and ½ cup light mayonnaise.

Grilled Marinated Vegetable Salad is easy to tote and tastes great served either chilled or at room temperature.

Grilled Marinated Vegetable Salad

MAKES 8 TO 10 SERVINGS
PREP: 35 MIN., GRILL: 14 MIN., CHILL: 8 HRS.

4 tablespoons olive oil, divided
3 tablespoons honey
2 tablespoons balsamic vinegar
1 teaspoon salt
½ teaspoon pepper
3 large yellow squash
3 large zucchini
2 medium-size green bell peppers
2 medium-size red bell peppers
2 medium-size orange bell peppers
2 medium-size yellow bell peppers
1 pound fresh green beans

STIR together 1 tablespoon oil, honey, and next 3 ingredients until blended. Set aside.

SLICE squash and zucchini; cut bell peppers into 1-inch pieces, and trim green beans. Toss squash, zucchini, and bell pepper with 2 tablespoons oil. Toss green beans with remaining 1 tablespoon oil.

GRILL squash, zucchini, and bell pepper in a grill wok, covered with grill lid, over medium-high heat (350° to 400°), stirring occasionally, 5 to 7 minutes or until vegetables are tender. Remove from wok.

GRILL green beans in grill wok, covered with grill lid, over medium-high heat, stirring occasionally, 5 to 7 minutes or until tender.

TOSS vegetables with honey mixture; cover and chill 8 hours.

New Potato Salad

MAKES 8 SERVINGS
PREP: 15 MIN., COOK: 30 MIN., CHILL: 8 HRS.

4 pounds new potatoes
¼ cup white vinegar
2 garlic cloves
1 teaspoon sugar
½ teaspoon salt
½ teaspoon pepper
¾ cup olive oil
2 tablespoons chopped fresh basil
2 pints grape tomatoes*
⅓ cup chopped red onion
8 bacon slices, cooked and crumbled

COOK potatoes in boiling water to cover 25 to 30 minutes or just until tender; drain and cool. Cut in half.

PROCESS vinegar and next 4 ingredients in a blender, stopping to scrape down sides. Turn blender on high, and gradually add oil in a slow, steady stream. Stir in chopped basil.

PLACE potato, tomatoes, and onion in a large bowl. Drizzle with dressing; toss gently. Cover and chill 8 hours. Top with crumbled bacon just before serving.

*Substitute 2 large tomatoes, seeded and chopped.

Creamy Dill Slaw

MAKES 8 SERVINGS
PREP: 10 MIN., CHILL: 8 HRS.

4 green onions, sliced
1 (8-ounce) container sour cream*
1 cup mayonnaise*
2 tablespoons sugar
2 tablespoons chopped fresh dill
2 tablespoons white vinegar
1 teaspoon salt
½ teaspoon pepper
1 (16-ounce) package coleslaw mix
1 (10-ounce) package finely shredded
  cabbage
Garnish: chopped fresh dill

STIR together first 8 ingredients in a large bowl until mixture is blended; stir in coleslaw mix and cabbage. Cover and chill 8 hours. Garnish, if desired.

Underneath a flaky top crust, Granny Smith apples lend tart sweetness to this classic pie. Scrumptious Chocolate-Glazed Brownies provide a quick, welcoming dessert (right).

*Substitute 1 (8-ounce) container light sour cream and 1 cup light mayonnaise.

Granny Smith Apple Pie

MAKES 8 SERVINGS
PREP: 30 MIN., BAKE: 50 MIN.

1½ (15-ounce) packages refrigerated piecrusts, divided
6 medium Granny Smith apples, peeled and sliced
1½ tablespoons lemon juice
¾ cup firmly packed brown sugar
½ cup granulated sugar
⅓ cup all-purpose flour
1 teaspoon ground cinnamon
½ teaspoon ground nutmeg

STACK 2 piecrusts; gently roll or press together. Fit pastry into a 9-inch deep-dish pieplate.
TOSS together apple and lemon juice in a large bowl. Combine brown sugar and next 4 ingredients; sprinkle over apple mixture, and toss to coat. Spoon into prepared piecrust.
ROLL remaining piecrust to press out fold lines; place over filling. Fold edges under, and crimp; cut slits in top for steam to escape.
BAKE at 450° for 15 minutes. Reduce oven temperature to 350°, and bake 35 minutes.

Chocolate-Glazed Brownies

MAKES 18 BROWNIES
PREP: 30 MIN., COOL: 15 MIN., BAKE: 30 MIN., STAND: 5 MIN.

1 cup sugar
⅔ cup butter or margarine
¼ cup water
4 cups semisweet chocolate morsels, divided
1 teaspoon vanilla extract
1½ cups all-purpose flour
½ teaspoon baking soda
½ teaspoon salt
4 large eggs
1 cup chopped pecans, toasted

STIR together first 3 ingredients in a large saucepan over high heat, stirring constantly, until sugar melts. Add 2 cups chocolate morsels and vanilla, and stir until mixture is smooth. Let cool 15 minutes.
ADD flour, baking soda, and salt to cooled chocolate mixture, and stir until blended. Stir in eggs and chopped pecans until blended. Spread brownie batter into a greased and floured 13- x 9-inch pan.
BAKE at 325° for 30 minutes. Sprinkle remaining 2 cups chocolate morsels evenly over warm brownies, and let stand 5 minutes to soften. Spread morsels over top. Cool on a wire rack.

Cook's Notes
■ Make the coleslaw, potato salad, grilled vegetable salad, pie, brownies, and lemonade the day before.
■ Roll the sandwiches the day of the picnic; or bring the ingredients with you, and let each person make his or her own.
■ Be sure all the food is cold before it goes into the cooler. Stock the cooler well with gel packs or large freezer bags filled with ice (don't forget extra ice for the drinks). For more food safety tips, turn to page 80.

The Ultimate Fish Fry

Gather your friends and family for this down-home feast of catfish with all the trimmings.

Few things are more Southern than a good old-fashioned catfish fry. Our Test Kitchens found 4- to 6-ounce, thin-cut fillets easy to manage in the Dutch oven, and they curl up when cooked, giving great eye appeal. As for condiments, use your favorite hot sauce, a dab of ketchup, tartar sauce, or a squeeze of lemon.

If you purchase frozen fillets, place them in a colander with a pan underneath, and thaw in the refrigerator overnight; otherwise, keep them in the coldest part of your refrigerator, and use within two days. When you buy the catfish, be sure to purchase American grain-fed catfish, not imported look-alike fish.

Creamy Sweet Slaw

MAKES 8 SERVINGS
PREP: 20 MIN.

½ cup sugar
¼ cup white vinegar
¾ cup mayonnaise
⅓ cup evaporated milk
1 teaspoon salt
½ teaspoon black pepper
1 large cabbage, shredded*
4 celery ribs, chopped
1 small green bell pepper, finely
  chopped
1 (2-ounce) jar diced pimiento, drained

STIR together first 6 ingredients in a large bowl; add cabbage and remaining ingredients, tossing to coat.
*2 (10-ounce) bags angel hair cabbage may be substituted for shredded cabbage.

Fried Catfish

MAKES 8 SERVINGS
PREP: 15 MIN., COOK: 12 MIN. PER BATCH

3 large eggs
½ cup milk
1 teaspoon salt
¼ teaspoon pepper
½ (1-pound) package saltines
8 catfish fillets (3½ to 4 pounds)
Vegetable oil

WHISK together first 4 ingredients; set aside. Process crackers in a food processor until finely crushed.
DIP fish in egg mixture; dredge in cracker crumbs.
POUR oil to a depth of 5 inches in a Dutch oven; heat to 375°.
FRY fish, in batches, 4 to 6 minutes on each side or until fish flakes with a fork. Drain on paper towels.

Buttermilk Hush Puppies

MAKES 5 DOZEN
PREP: 20 MIN., COOK: 7 MIN. PER BATCH

2 cups self-rising flour
2 cups self-rising white cornmeal
1 teaspoon sugar
½ teaspoon salt
½ teaspoon pepper
1 large onion, grated
1 jalapeño pepper (optional), seeded and
  minced
2 cups buttermilk
1 large egg
Vegetable oil

COMBINE first 5 ingredients in a large bowl; stir in onion and, if desired, jalapeño.
WHISK together buttermilk and egg; add to flour mixture.
POUR oil to a depth of 3 inches in a Dutch oven; heat to 375°.

DROP batter by level tablespoonfuls into oil; fry in batches 5 to 7 minutes or until golden. Drain on paper towels.

Home-Style Baked Beans

MAKES 6 TO 8 SERVINGS
PREP: 10 MIN., BAKE: 46 MIN.

2 (28-ounce) cans baked beans with tangy
  sauce, bacon, and brown sugar
1 sweet onion, quartered
1 cup ketchup
½ to ¾ cup prepared mustard
2 tablespoons light brown sugar
4 bacon slices

STIR together first 5 ingredients; pour into a lightly greased 11- x 7-inch baking dish. Top with bacon.
BAKE, uncovered, at 400° for 45 minutes. Broil 5 inches from heat 1 minute or until bacon is brown.
NOTE: For testing purposes only, we used Bush's Original Baked Beans.

Fried Catfish, Home-Style Baked Beans, Creamy Sweet Slaw, and Buttermilk Hush Puppies

Casual Supper Club Gathering

Hosting your supper club is a cinch with these make-ahead recipes and doable decorating ideas.

Sharing good times with good friends is one of life's basic pleasures. Joining a supper club makes that pleasure a frequent occurrence. It's a great way to make new friends, keep up with old ones, get to know your neighbors, or merely satisfy the urge to cook and entertain.

Supper club formats are flexible. Some meet during the week, while others find weekends more relaxing. Some clubs create themed dinners; others keep it simple. Many include significant others or children, while some are for ladies (or guys) only.

You don't need a large dining room or lavishly appointed kitchen to host a supper club. For a large group, plan a casual menu suitable for eating in the living room or backyard. If your kitchen is small, prepare some dishes the day before or make the occasion a potluck so other members can help with the cooking.

However your group decides to structure its gatherings, let this simple menu inspire you to join a supper club or start one in your neighborhood. This casual bill of fare generously serves a party of eight. Good food lays the foundation for good times with good friends.

Make-Ahead
Supper Club Menu
Serves 8
Baked Vidalia Onion Dip
Italian Pot Roast
Bacon-Mandarin Salad
Roasted Zucchini
Mocha Cake
Chocolate Martinis
Iced tea

Both the original and light versions of Baked Vidalia Onion Dip earn rave reviews from guests.

Baked Vidalia Onion Dip

MAKES 12 SERVINGS
PREP: 15 MIN., BAKE: 25 MIN., STAND: 10 MIN.

2 tablespoons butter or margarine
3 large Vidalia onions, coarsely chopped
2 cups (8 ounces) shredded Swiss cheese
2 cups mayonnaise
1 (8-ounce) can sliced water chestnuts, drained and chopped
¼ cup dry white wine
1 garlic clove, minced
½ teaspoon hot sauce

MELT butter in a large skillet over medium-high heat; add onion, and sauté 10 minutes or until tender.

STIR together shredded Swiss cheese and next 5 ingredients; stir in onion, blending well. Spoon mixture into a lightly greased 2-quart baking dish.

BAKE at 375° for 25 minutes; remove from oven, and let stand 10 minutes. Serve with tortilla chips or crackers.

TO LIGHTEN: Substitute vegetable cooking spray for butter; use reduced-fat Swiss cheese and light mayonnaise.

Italian Pot Roast

MAKES 6 TO 8 SERVINGS
PREP: 35 MIN.; COOK: 3 HRS., 38 MIN.

To make ahead, chill baked roast overnight. Cut into thin slices, and place in a 13- x 9-inch baking dish. Top with gravy. Bake at 350° for 30 minutes or until thoroughly heated. Serve with roasted potatoes.

1 (4½-pound) rib-eye roast, trimmed*
2 tablespoons vegetable oil
1 (15-ounce) can tomato sauce
½ cup red wine
2 large tomatoes, chopped
1 medium onion, minced
4 garlic cloves, minced
1 tablespoon salt
1 tablespoon pepper
2 teaspoons chopped fresh or 1 teaspoon dried basil
2 teaspoons chopped fresh or 1 teaspoon dried oregano
1 (16-ounce) package red potatoes, cut into wedges
½ teaspoon salt
¼ teaspoon pepper
3 tablespoons all-purpose flour
1 cup beef broth or water
Garnish: chopped fresh parsley

COOK roast in hot oil in a large Dutch oven over medium-high heat 5 to 6 minutes or until browned on all sides.

COMBINE tomato sauce and next 8 ingredients; pour sauce mixture over roast in Dutch oven.

BAKE, covered, at 325° for 3 hours or until roast is tender. Remove roast from Dutch oven, and keep warm; reserve drippings in Dutch oven.

PLACE potato wedges in a lightly greased 15- x 10-inch jellyroll pan. Bake at 450° for 30 minutes. Sprinkle with ½ teaspoon salt and ¼ teaspoon pepper.

SKIM fat from drippings in Dutch oven. Whisk together flour and beef broth until smooth; add to drippings. Cook mixture, stirring constantly, over low heat 8 minutes or until thickened.

CUT roast into thin slices. Arrange roast and potatoes on a serving platter. Garnish, if desired. Serve with tomato gravy.

*One 4½-pound boneless beef rump roast, trimmed, can be substituted. Bake, covered, at 325° for 2 hours and 20 minutes or until tender.

Bacon-Mandarin Salad

MAKES 12 SERVINGS
PREP: 15 MIN., COOK: 18 MIN.

Wash the lettuces the night before. Wrap the leaves in a damp paper towel, and chill in zip-top plastic bags. Cook the bacon, and toast the almonds ahead, too. Assemble and dress the salad right before serving.

½ cup olive oil
¼ cup red wine vinegar
¼ cup sugar
1 tablespoon chopped fresh basil
⅛ teaspoon hot sauce
2 (15-ounce) cans mandarin oranges, drained and chilled*
1 bunch Red Leaf lettuce, torn
1 head romaine lettuce, torn
1 (16-ounce) package bacon, cooked and crumbled
1 (4-ounce) package sliced almonds, toasted

Bacon-Mandarin Salad

WHISK together first 5 ingredients in a large bowl, blending well. Add oranges and lettuces, tossing gently to coat. Sprinkle with crumbled bacon and sliced almonds. Serve immediately.

*Fresh orange segments can be substituted for canned mandarin oranges, if desired.

Roasted Zucchini

MAKES 12 SERVINGS
PREP: 10 MIN., BAKE: 30 MIN., COOK: 4 MIN.

If you don't have sesame oil, olive oil will work just fine.

4 pounds zucchini, sliced
¼ cup sesame oil, divided
1 (12-ounce) jar roasted red bell peppers, drained and coarsely chopped
½ cup coarsely chopped walnuts
½ teaspoon ground ginger or 1 teaspoon minced fresh ginger
2 garlic cloves, minced
¼ teaspoon dried crushed red pepper
¼ cup chicken broth
¼ cup soy sauce
½ to 1 teaspoon sugar

ARRANGE zucchini in an aluminum foil-lined jellyroll pan; drizzle with 2 tablespoons sesame oil.
BAKE at 475° for 30 minutes, turning once.
SAUTÉ bell pepper and next 4 ingredients in remaining 2 tablespoons hot sesame oil in a large skillet over medium-high heat 2 minutes. Reduce heat to medium. Stir in chicken broth, soy sauce, and sugar; cook until thoroughly heated. Serve over zucchini.

"Plan an after-dinner activity, such as a board game, movie, or even a walk around the block. It's a great way to strengthen bonds between your members."

Debbie Mason
Valrico, Florida

Easy Ideas for Hosting Friends

You're more likely to enjoy playing host if you have an organized plan of action. Calm preparty jitters with these hints.

■ Choose decorative table linens to create a seasonal setting.
■ Dishes with busy patterns often pair best with solid-colored napkins, and vice versa. You can mix and match different-colored napkins, then embellish the place setting with a fresh flower or fresh herb sprig.
■ Turn place mats vertically for a unique setting and to make room for more guests at the table.
■ Lay out serving pieces and utensils ahead so they'll be handy when the food is ready to serve.

■ Tie a bunch of flowers to rear legs of chairs to denote a place of honor, the host's chair, or perhaps all the ladies' places.
■ For a potluck, use sticky notes or tape to label each dish on the underside with the name of the person who brought it.
■ Pick up fresh flowers the day before. Prepare them by stripping the leaves, cutting the stems at an angle under cool running water, and soaking the stems overnight in a cool place.

■ Create a low centerpiece for your table. If you're unsure about the height of an arrangement you've made, sit down at the table to verify that it won't obstruct your view of other diners. For a long table, use several petite arrangements, placing a few blooms in small vases spaced along the length of the table.
■ Garnish each glass with sprigs of rosemary woven around the base. The day before, run cut sprigs under cool water; wrap sprigs in damp paper towels, and store in the refrigerator until you're ready to decorate wine stems.

"Capture memorable supper club moments in a scrapbook or a recipe collection. Include favorite photos, invitations, and menus. We published a cookbook celebrating 38 years of dining together."

The Supper Club
Dallas, Texas

Mocha Cake

MAKES 1 (10-INCH) CAKE
PREP: 25 MIN., BAKE: 55 MIN., COOL: 15 MIN.

2 cups sour cream
2 large eggs
1 (18.25-ounce) package chocolate cake mix
½ cup coffee liqueur
¼ cup vegetable oil
2 cups semisweet chocolate morsels
½ cup crushed almond toffee bits (optional)
Powdered sugar
1 pint whipping cream
¼ cup powdered sugar

STIR together first 5 ingredients in a large bowl; blend well. Stir in morsels and, if desired, toffee bits. Pour batter into a greased and floured 10-inch Bundt pan.
BAKE at 350° for 50 to 55 minutes or until a wooden pick inserted in center comes out clean. Cool in pan on a wire rack 10 to 15 minutes; remove from pan, and cool completely on wire rack. Sprinkle with powdered sugar.
BEAT whipping cream at medium speed with an electric mixer until foamy; gradually add ¼ cup powdered sugar, beating until soft peaks form. Serve with cake.
NOTE: For testing purposes only, we used Kahlúa coffee liqueur and Heath Bits 'O Brickle Almond Toffee Bits for crushed almond toffee bits.

Chocolate Martinis

MAKES 10 TO 12 SERVINGS
PREP: 15 MIN., STAND: 5 MIN., CHILL: 1 HR.

2 to 2½ cups vodka, chilled
1¼ cups chocolate liqueur
¼ cup raspberry liqueur
¼ cup half-and-half (optional)
Chocolate liqueur or syrup
Sweetened cocoa

STIR together vodka, liqueurs, and, if desired, half-and-half in a large pitcher; chill at least 1 hour.
FILL martini glasses with ice. Let stand 5 minutes; discard ice.
DIP rims of chilled glasses in chocolate liqueur; then dip in cocoa, coating rims. Pour vodka mixture into glasses. Serve immediately.
NOTE: For testing purposes only, we used Godiva Liqueur for chocolate liqueur, Chambord for raspberry liqueur, and Ghirardelli Sweet Ground Chocolate and Cocoa for sweetened cocoa.

INDIVIDUAL CHOCOLATE MARTINI:
In a martini shaker, combine ¼ cup vodka, 2 tablespoons chocolate liqueur, 1½ teaspoons raspberry liqueur, 6 ice cubes, and, if desired, a dash of half-and-half. Cover with lid; shake until thoroughly chilled. Remove lid; strain into a chilled martini glass. Serve immediately. Makes 1 serving.

Start a Supper Club

Ready to have a group at your house? These suggestions from supper clubbers around the South will help you host a fabulous mixer with friends.

■ When we relocated to Florida, I decided to host a kick-off breakfast with a few interested neighbors. If you're starting up a group like this, my advice is to center your first planning meeting around a theme and menu ideas, dietary restrictions, monthly schedules, and general guidelines. The predetermined schedule and dish assignments make organizing monthly dinners a lot easier and leave little room for confusion.

Cheryl Howlin
Fairway Hills Supper Club
Lake Mary, FL

■ Agree on a theme with your group, and assign each member a recipe. This allows everyone to enjoy the planning and preparation.

Nancy Kimberly
Birmingham, AL

Chocolate Martinis Step-by-Step

■ Fill martini glass with ice to chill; set aside.
■ Prepare martini as directed; cover shaker with lid, and shake until thoroughly chilled.
■ Discard ice from glass, shaking out excess. Dip glass rim in chocolate liqueur; then dip in sweetened cocoa, coating rim well. Remove shaker lid, and strain mixture into prepared glass.

"While most supper clubs are all-adult events, consider inviting children to an occasional meeting. Around the holidays, we host a supper club for the kids. We let them plan the menu, and each child gets to prepare his or her dish."

Lynn Gardner
Memphis, Tennessee

Mocha Cake

Step Into the Garden

Extend a gracious invitation to wonderful food and an extraordinary place.

Lucinda Hutson's garden is something of a legend in Austin. An invitation from Lucinda, an authority on ethnic herbs and an accomplished cook, brings a guaranteed fiesta. You may be encouraged to garnish your salad from the kitchen bed, or add a splash of color to your sangría from any number of flowering herbs. "You can browse through the garden and add different flavors to your meal. I like people to interact with the garden," she says. One thing is certain—your hostess will welcome you with a gracious mix of Southern charm and Hispanic culture.

Space, Color, and Style

Color is a celebration in Lucinda's garden. The untraditional house color—purple—and garage-turned-garden-shed are a throwback to Hispanic culture and family. "In Mexico, houses are painted bright colors—many times they're turquoise, hot pink, or canary yellow. I wanted a strong color, and purple was my grandmother's favorite. She wore purple, and everything she owned was purple. She was the purple lady. So in a funny way, it's in homage to Grandmother," she says.

Style is Lucinda's forte, along with her easygoing flair for detail. Each garden room is furnished with artifacts collected from south-of-the-border trips and gifts from local artist friends. A joyful mix of Hispanic terra-cotta ornaments, mosaics, and folk art make each space unique. "My garden is such a personal place, filled with special things my friends have made and memories of my travels. They are as important to the garden as the flowers and herbs," she says.

Kitchen and Garden In One Festive World

Lucinda's kitchen comes alive with the smells, flavors, and celebratory spirit of the Southwestern and Hispanic cultures she holds so dear. "Don't be surprised to find garlic and chile peppers in most of my recipes," says Lucinda. "After all, they're as inherent to the Southwest as sunshine." And her gusto for entertaining and cooking is best exemplified in her recipes (see pages 56-57). "I don't want people to have to be in the kitchen all day. When I entertain, it's usually in the garden, so I try to keep things simple, relying on bold flavors and garnishes to be especially festive, colorful, and fun," she explains.

Lucinda's Sage Advice On Herbs

- Herbs are best gathered midmorning, when the dew has dried, but before the sun saps the natural oils.
- When working with herbs in the kitchen, always use a sharp knife and work quickly, because herbs darken and bruise easily.
- Herbs such as mint, basil, parsley, and cilantro can be stored several days in a jar with water covering just the stems. Change the water daily, and store in a cool place away from direct sunlight.

- For soups and stews, add herbs during the last 10 to 15 minutes of cooking to retain their flavor and prevent bitterness.
- Citrus juices, wine, and vinegar often cause herbs to darken or fade. So when making salad dressings, add herbs just before serving.

Lucinda uses color to enhance the garden's Mexican atmosphere. The purple house is a loving tribute to her grandmother—"the purple lady."

Lucinda's unique take on sangría, the Latin wine cooler, makes a refreshing treat on a summer afternoon. Basil-Cheese Torta (below) makes a beautiful presentation and a delicious garden-party treat.

Garden Sangría

MAKES 1½ GALLONS
PREP: 10 MIN., CHILL: 8 HRS.

1 gallon dry white wine
2 cups brandy
1 cup orange liqueur
4 oranges, sliced
1 bunch fresh mint leaves
1 (1-liter) bottle club soda, chilled*
1 quart whole strawberries
2 lemons, thinly sliced
2 limes, thinly sliced
Garnishes: fresh mint sprigs, strawberries, red seedless grapes, orange and lime wedges

COMBINE first 5 ingredients in a large container; cover and chill 8 hours.
ADD club soda and next 3 ingredients just before serving; serve over ice, if desired. Garnish, if desired.
*Substitute ginger ale for club soda.

Basil-Cheese Torta

MAKES 12 SERVINGS
PREP: 40 MIN., CHILL: 8 HRS.

1 (8-ounce) package cream cheese, softened
1 (4-ounce) package feta cheese
2 tablespoons butter or margarine, softened
Lucinda's Garden Pesto
2 (6-ounce) packages provolone cheese slices, divided
Roasted Red Pepper Salsa, divided
¼ cup chopped pine nuts, toasted
Garnishes: fresh basil sprigs, pine nuts

PROCESS first 3 ingredients in a blender or food processor until smooth, stopping to scrape down sides. Stir in pesto, blending well.
LINE an 8- x 4-inch loafpan with plastic wrap, allowing 1 inch to hang over each side.

ARRANGE one-third of cheese slices on bottom and up sides of pan.

LAYER evenly with half of pesto mixture, 1/3 cup Roasted Red Pepper Salsa, and 2 tablespoons pine nuts; top with half of remaining cheese slices. Repeat layers, ending with cheese slices, and gently press. Fold cheese slices toward center. Cover and chill 8 hours.

INVERT torta onto a serving platter. Top with 1/3 cup salsa; garnish, if desired. Serve with remaining salsa and toasted French baguette slices.

Lucinda's Garden Pesto:

MAKES 1 CUP
PREP: 10 MIN.

3 cups fresh basil leaves
4 to 6 garlic cloves
1/2 cup pine nuts, walnuts, or pecans
3/4 cup shredded Parmesan cheese
2 to 3 tablespoons shredded Romano cheese
2/3 cup olive oil

PROCESS basil and garlic in a food processor until chopped. Add pine nuts and cheeses, and process until blended, stopping to scrape down sides. With processor running, pour oil through food chute in a slow, steady stream; process until smooth. Chill up to 5 days, if desired.

Roasted Red Pepper Salsa:

MAKES 2 CUPS
PREP: 20 MIN., BAKE: 12 MIN., STAND: 13 MIN.

4 red bell peppers
1 tablespoon olive oil
1/2 cup dried tomatoes*
3 tablespoons chopped fresh basil
1 tablespoon balsamic vinegar
2 to 3 garlic cloves, minced
1/2 teaspoon salt
1/2 teaspoon finely chopped fresh rosemary
1/4 teaspoon ground red pepper

BAKE peppers on an aluminum foil-lined baking sheet at 500° for 12 minutes or until peppers look blistered, turning once.

PLACE peppers in a zip-top freezer bag; seal and let stand 10 minutes to loosen skins. Peel peppers; remove and discard seeds. Coarsely chop peppers.

DRIZZLE with 1 tablespoon olive oil; set aside.

POUR boiling water to cover over dried tomatoes. Let stand 3 minutes; drain and coarsely chop.

STIR together bell peppers, tomato, basil, and remaining ingredients. Cover and chill salsa up to 2 days, if desired.

*Substitute 1/3 cup dried tomatoes in oil for dried tomatoes. Drain tomatoes well, pressing between layers of paper towels.

Garlic-and-Rosemary Shrimp

MAKES 4 SERVINGS
PREP: 20 MIN., COOK: 10 MIN.

Use this recipe as an appetizer or a main dish served over pasta.

1 pound unpeeled, medium-size fresh shrimp
2 tablespoons butter or margarine
1/4 cup extra-virgin olive oil
1 large garlic bulb
1/2 cup dry white wine
2 tablespoons white wine vinegar
1 tablespoon lemon juice
2 tablespoons chopped fresh rosemary
1 teaspoon dried oregano
1 teaspoon salt
1/2 teaspoon dried crushed red pepper
3 dried red chile peppers
3 bay leaves
Garnishes: lemon slices, red chile peppers, fresh rosemary sprigs

PEEL shrimp, leaving tails on; devein, if desired, and set aside.

MELT butter with oil in a large skillet over medium-high heat. Cut garlic bulb in half crosswise; separate and peel cloves. Add to butter mixture; sauté 2 minutes.

STIR in wine and next 8 ingredients; cook, stirring constantly, 1 minute or until thoroughly heated.

ADD shrimp; cook 3 to 5 minutes or just until shrimp turn pink. Garnish, if desired.

NOTE: If serving over pasta, remove and discard bay leaves.

Garlic-and-Rosemary Shrimp

It's a Special Occasion

*Celebrate a birthday (or new job
or a loved one's homecoming)
with a feast of fall's finest foods and flavors.*

Shorter days, cooler nights, and leaves turning amber and burnt red are a call to gather friends for a fall dinner—especially if there's a reason—like a special birthday. The menu and decorations themselves are celebrations of fabulous foods and seasonal flowers. When the birthday guy or girl blows out the candles on one of our two divine cake choices, he or she will be wishing for a party like this one every year.

A Celebration Supper
Serves 4 to 6

Start the party with one of these:

Orange Pecans and assorted
Cheddar cheeses

or

Sweet Potato Fritters With
Peanut Dipping Sauce

or

Roasted Butternut Squash-and-
Apple Bisque

Serve a dinner of:

Hot 'n' Sweet Glazed Pork Chops

Tossed white and wild rice

Steamed green beans

Two-Seed Bread Knots

Blow out the candles on:

German Chocolate-Apple Cake

or

Banana Split Cake

Nestle the celebration dessert, German-Chocolate Apple Cake, among the fall decorations. A fresh flower wreath leaning against the wall is a unique way to add flowers without taking up space.

Orange Pecans complement an assortment of Cheddar cheeses. Make it simple—offer an extra sharp, a white, and one layered with another cheese, such as blue.

Orange Pecans

MAKES ABOUT 5 CUPS
PREP: 10 MIN., COOK: 10 MIN.

Send a present home with each guest. Package pecans in plastic bags, and tie with a festive bow. Include an idea on the gift tag:"Try these pecans sprinkled over a green salad tossed with orange segments and vinaigrette dressing."

1 cup sugar
1¼ cups fresh orange juice
1 tablespoon grated orange rind
1 teaspoon ground cinnamon
4 cups pecan halves, toasted

BRING first 4 ingredients to a rapid boil in a heavy saucepan over medium heat. Stir in pecan halves; cook, stirring constantly, until pecans are coated and syrup is absorbed. Remove from heat; stir just until pecans separate. Spread in a single layer onto wax paper; cool. Store in airtight containers.

Sweet Potato Fritters With Peanut Dipping Sauce

MAKES 4 DOZEN
PREP: 10 MIN., FRY: 3 MIN. PER BATCH

To keep fritters warm but not soggy on the bottom, place on a wire rack over a baking sheet; keep in a 200° oven.

2½ cups self-rising flour
1 cup self-rising yellow cornmeal
2 tablespoons sugar
¾ teaspoon ground ginger
¼ teaspoon ground cinnamon
¼ teaspoon ground nutmeg
2¼ cups peeled, cubed, and cooked sweet
    potatoes (about 1 pound uncooked)
2 cups buttermilk
3 large eggs
Peanut oil
Peanut Dipping Sauce

COMBINE first 6 ingredients in a large bowl; stir in sweet potatoes.
WHISK together buttermilk and eggs. Add to flour mixture, stirring mixture just until moistened.
POUR oil to a depth of 1 inch into a deep cast-iron skillet; heat to 350°.
DROP dough, in batches, by rounded tablespoonfuls into hot oil, and fry 1½ minutes on each side or until golden brown. Drain well on paper towels, and serve with Peanut Dipping Sauce.

Peanut Dipping Sauce:

MAKES ABOUT 1¼ CUPS
PREP: 5 MIN.

½ cup creamy peanut butter
⅓ cup orange juice
¼ cup orange marmalade
¼ teaspoon ground red pepper
¼ teaspoon salt
¼ cup water

PROCESS first 5 ingredients in a food processor until smooth, stopping to scrape down sides. With processor running, add water in a slow, steady stream through food chute; process until smooth.

Sweet Potato Fritters With Peanut Dipping Sauce

Roasted Butternut Squash-and-Apple Bisque

MAKES ABOUT 2½ QUARTS
PREP: 20 MIN., BAKE: 30 MIN., COOK: 35 MIN.

Garnish individual bowls of this thick soup with a drizzle of half-and-half and toasted sunflower kernels, if desired.

2 (1½-pound) butternut squash, peeled and
    cut into 1-inch pieces
Vegetable cooking spray
1 tablespoon butter or margarine
4 large Granny Smith apples, peeled and
    chopped
1 large sweet onion, diced
2½ teaspoons ground curry powder
1 teaspoon ground ginger
¼ teaspoon ground cinnamon
4 cups chicken broth
1 cup regular or fat-free half-and-half

ARRANGE squash in a single layer in a lightly greased 15- x 10-inch jellyroll pan; lightly coat squash with cooking spray.
BAKE at 475° for 30 minutes. Remove from oven; set aside.
MELT the butter in a stockpot over medium-high heat; add apples and onion, and sauté 10 minutes. Stir in curry powder, ginger, and cinnamon, and cook 1 to 2 minutes.
STIR in squash and chicken broth, and bring to a boil. Reduce heat, and simmer, stirring occasionally, 15 minutes. Remove from heat.
PROCESS squash mixture, in batches, in a blender or food processor until smooth, stopping to scrape down sides.
RETURN squash mixture to stockpot; stir in half-and-half, and cook, stirring constantly, over medium heat until thoroughly heated.

Hot 'n' Sweet Glazed Pork Chops

MAKES 4 TO 6 SERVINGS
PREP: 10 MIN., CHILL: 1 HR., COOK: 11 MIN.

½ cup seasoned rice wine vinegar, divided
½ cup orange juice, divided
1 tablespoon Chinese five spice
3 tablespoons sesame oil, divided
8 (4-ounce) boneless center-cut pork chops
1 (12-ounce) container cranberry-orange
    relish
¼ cup sugar
1 teaspoon ground ginger
1 teaspoon ground ancho chile pepper
4 green onions, sliced

COMBINE ¼ cup vinegar, ¼ cup orange juice, Chinese five spice, and 2 tablespoons sesame oil in a shallow dish or large zip-top freezer bag; add pork chops. Cover or seal, and chill at least 1 hour, turning once.

BRING remaining ¼ cup vinegar, remaining ¼ cup orange juice, cranberry-orange relish, and next 3 ingredients to a boil in a heavy 3-quart saucepan over medium-high heat. Boil, whisking often, 5 minutes. Remove from heat, and set aside.

REMOVE pork chops from marinade; discard marinade.

BROWN pork chops in remaining 1 tablespoon oil in a large nonstick skillet over medium-high heat 1 to 2 minutes on each side. Add cranberry mixture; bring to a boil, and cook 1 to 2 minutes or until pork chops are glazed and thoroughly cooked. Sprinkle with green onions, and serve immediately.

NOTE: For testing purposes only, we used Ocean Spray Cran-Fruit For Chicken (Cranberry Orange Crushed Fruit) for the cranberry-orange relish and McCormick Gourmet Collection Ancho Chile Pepper.

Cranberry-orange relish and ground ancho chile pepper are the secret ingredients in Hot 'n' Sweet Glazed Pork Chops.

How to Shape Two-Seed Bread Knots

1. Roll each ball of dough into a 7-inch rope.
2. Twist dough around fingers.
3. Pull end of rope through center to form a knot.
Note: Cover dough with plastic wrap or a clean towel to keep it from drying out. A pastry scraper (left in photos) makes cutting and working with the dough much easier.

Two-Seed Bread Knots

MAKES 20 ROLLS
PREP: 30 MIN., STAND: 5 MIN., RISE: 20 MIN., BAKE: 17 MIN.

Most yeast rolls require two risings of the dough, but this recipe needs only one.

1 (¼-ounce) envelope rapid-rise yeast
1 cup warm water (100° to 110°)
3½ cups bread flour
2 tablespoons sugar
1½ teaspoons salt
3 tablespoons olive oil
1 egg yolk
1 tablespoon water
1 tablespoon sesame seeds
1 teaspoon poppy seeds

PREHEAT oven to 200°. Combine yeast and 1 cup warm water in a 1-cup liquid measuring cup; let stand 5 minutes.

COMBINE flour, sugar, and salt in a heavy-duty mixing bowl. Add yeast mixture and oil. Beat at low speed with an electric mixer 1 minute; beat at medium speed 5 minutes.

DIVIDE dough into 20 equal balls. Roll each ball into a 7-inch rope, and twist into a knot. Combine egg yolk and 1 tablespoon water; brush over rolls. Sprinkle with seeds; place on parchment paper-lined baking sheets. Turn off oven, and cover rolls loosely with plastic wrap; place in oven, and let rise 15 to 20 minutes or until doubled in bulk. Remove from oven, and preheat oven to 400°. Discard plastic wrap.

BAKE at 400° for 15 to 17 minutes or until golden.

German Chocolate-Apple Cake

MAKES 10 TO 12 SERVINGS
PREP: 30 MIN., CHILL: 4 HRS., BAKE: 18 MIN.,
COOL: 10 MIN.

To chill quickly, place bowl of apple mixture in a larger bowl filled with ice. Stir often until mixture is completely cold and thickened.

1 (12-ounce) package frozen spiced apples
1½ cups firmly packed light brown sugar
¼ cup cornstarch
1 (12-ounce) can evaporated milk
3 large eggs
½ cup butter, melted
2 cups sweetened flaked coconut
1 cup coarsely chopped pecans, toasted
1 teaspoon vanilla extract
1 (18.25-ounce) package German chocolate
  cake mix
Garnish: pecan halves

COOK apples in microwave at HIGH 5 to 6 minutes. Let stand 2 minutes.

STIR together brown sugar and cornstarch in a heavy 3-quart saucepan; whisk in milk, eggs, and melted butter. Bring to a boil over medium heat, whisking constantly; boil 1 minute. (Mixture will thicken to a puddinglike consistency.) Remove from heat; stir in apples, coconut, pecans, and vanilla.

SPOON mixture into a bowl. Place a sheet of wax paper directly on surface of mixture to prevent a film from forming; chill at least 4 hours.

PREPARE cake mix according to package directions. Spoon batter evenly into 3 greased and floured 9-inch round cakepans.

BAKE at 350° for 18 minutes or until a wooden pick inserted in center comes out clean. Cool in pans on wire racks 10 minutes. Remove from pans, and cool completely on wire racks.

SPREAD chilled apple mixture between layers and on top of cake. Serve immediately, or chill, if desired. Garnish, if desired.

NOTE: For testing purposes only, we used Stouffer's Harvest Apples for the frozen spiced apples.

Floral Accents

Large floral arrangements can overwhelm a table, especially one with limited space. For compact beauty and big impact, decorate with water goblets topped with rose kissing balls. Use one for a card-table size seating, or line up three or more down the center of a rectangular table.

To make your own kissing ball, soak a 4-inch sphere of florist foam (available at florist or craft stores) in water. Cut stems of small budded roses and Brunia (the green berries) about 3 inches below blooms and berries, and push into foam. Leave a rounded space without flowers for foam to rest on top of water goblet.

To make a wreath, choose a florist foam wreath form in a size proportionate to your sideboard and other accessories. Soak as directed for kissing balls, and use Fuji mums, lime-green Kermit mums, and Solidago in addition to roses and Brunia. Send the wreath home with the honoree to hang on a door or window.

You'll want to offer vanilla ice cream and hot fudge sauce with each slice of this Banana Split Cake.

Banana Split Cake

MAKES 10 TO 12 SERVINGS
PREP: 30 MIN., BAKE: 1 HR., COOL: 15 MIN.

Use ripe, brown-speckled bananas for the sweetest flavor and easy mashing.

3 cups all-purpose flour
2 cups granulated sugar
1 teaspoon baking soda
¼ teaspoon salt
3 large eggs
1 cup vegetable oil
½ cup buttermilk
2 cups mashed bananas (5 medium)
1 cup chopped pecans
1 cup sweetened flaked coconut
1½ teaspoons vanilla extract
1 (20-ounce) can crushed pineapple, undrained
1 (16-ounce) jar maraschino cherries, drained
1 (8-ounce) package cream cheese, softened
1½ cups powdered sugar
Garnishes: toasted flaked coconut, long-stemmed maraschino cherries, grated milk chocolate, chopped pecans, hot fudge sauce

COMBINE first 4 ingredients in a large bowl. Stir together eggs, oil, and buttermilk. Add oil mixture to flour mixture, stirring just until dry ingredients are moistened. Stir in banana and next 3 ingredients.

DRAIN pineapple, reserving 2 tablespoons liquid. Gently press pineapple and cherries from jar between layers of paper towels to drain. Chop cherries. Stir pineapple and cherries into banana mixture. Spoon into a greased and floured 10-inch tube pan.

BAKE at 350° for 1 hour or until a wooden pick inserted in center comes out clean. Cool in pan on a wire rack 10 to 15 minutes; remove from pan, and cool on wire rack.

BEAT cream cheese at medium speed with an electric mixer until smooth. Gradually add powdered sugar, beating at low speed until blended. Stir in reserved pineapple juice. Pour over cake; garnish, if desired.

Week at the Beach

Five Suppers

The first two days you'll grill enough meat and poultry for the entire week. Afterward, you can switch the order of the meals to suit your schedule and taste.

Serves 6

Day 1: Peppery Grilled Flank Steak

Day 2: Chicken Fajitas

Day 3: Cheesy Tomato Pie

Day 4: Beef Salad Niçoise

Day 5: Quick Chicken Tostadas

Enjoy a last long weekend at the beach with this make-it-easy menu plan.
Round out each meal with bake-shop treats, and sip on a cool beverage as the sun goes down.

Summer may be officially over, but there's plenty of sunshine and surf to be enjoyed at the beach in early fall. Lower prices, smaller crowds, and brilliant skies entice you to extend an invitation to gather family and friends for one last golden weekend of the season. You'll want to enjoy every possible moment, so follow this strategy for five satisfying meals that feed about six and are easy to prepare and double as needed.

As you plan your trip, use our Ingredients List to pack your pantry staples, then take the list to your market to shop for perishables. En route, pick up produce from roadside stands, or keep an eye out for pick-your-own fields. Let everyone share the cooking duties—easy when all the ingredients and recipes are on hand. While the others are busy, you can relax on a chaise with a good book. You may even fall asleep caressed by the warm breeze and the sound of the surf.

Peppery Grilled Flank Steak

MAKES 6 SERVINGS
PREP: 10 MIN., CHILL: 8 HRS., GRILL: 16 MIN.

This recipe makes enough flank steak for two meals. On the first night, serve with steamed zucchini and grilled corn on the cob. Serve the remaining beef on Beef Salad Niçoise, page 66.

⅔ cup dry white wine
¼ cup olive oil
2½ tablespoons cracked pepper
4 teaspoons sugar
2 garlic cloves, pressed
2 red bell peppers, cut into thin strips
2 yellow bell peppers, cut into thin strips
2 (1½-pound) flank steaks, trimmed
Tomato-Cheese Bread

COMBINE first 7 ingredients in a shallow dish or large zip-top plastic freezer bag; add steaks. Cover or seal, and chill 8 hours, turning occasionally.
REMOVE steaks and bell pepper strips from marinade, discarding marinade. Place bell pepper strips in a grill basket.

(left) Although Cheesy Tomato Pie's presentation is gourmet, the recipe is as simple to make as a quiche.

GRILL steaks and bell pepper strips, covered with grill lid, over high heat (400° to 500°) 8 minutes on each side or to desired degree of doneness. Cut 1 flank steak diagonally across the grain into thin strips (reserve remaining flank steak for Beef Salad Niçoise). Serve sliced steak and bell pepper strips with Tomato-Cheese Bread.

Tomato-Cheese Bread:

MAKES 6 SERVINGS
PREP: 8 MIN., BROIL: 5 MIN.

1 (8-ounce) container soft cream cheese
¼ cup shredded Parmesan cheese
1 garlic clove, pressed
2 tablespoons chopped fresh basil
¼ teaspoon salt
⅛ teaspoon pepper
1 (16-ounce) French bread loaf
2 plum tomatoes, sliced

MICROWAVE cream cheese in a 1-quart microwave-safe bowl at HIGH 20 seconds. Stir in Parmesan cheese and next 4 ingredients.
CUT bread in half lengthwise; spread cream cheese mixture over cut sides of bread. Top with tomato slices. Place on a baking sheet, cut side up.
BROIL 5½ inches from heat 4 to 5 minutes. Cut into slices.

Friends and family munch on chips and salsa before a meal or as an afternoon snack.

Beef Salad Niçoise

FIT piecrust into a 9-inch deep-dish tart pan; prick bottom and sides of piecrust with a fork.

BAKE at 425° for 10 minutes. Remove from oven; set aside.

SAUTÉ bell pepper, onion, and garlic in hot oil in a large skillet 5 minutes or until tender; stir in basil.

WHISK together eggs and next 3 ingredients in a large bowl; stir in sautéed vegetables and cheeses. Pour into crust; top with tomato slices.

BAKE at 375° for 45 to 50 minutes or until set, shielding edges with strips of aluminum foil after 30 minutes to prevent excessive browning. Let stand 5 minutes before serving.

Chicken Fajitas

MAKES 6 SERVINGS
PREP: 10 MIN., CHILL: 2 HRS., GRILL: 25 MIN.

Spicy salsa, tortilla chips, drinks on ice, and chocolate cookies complete the meal.

1 cup vegetable oil
½ cup lime juice
½ cup chopped fresh cilantro
4 garlic cloves, pressed
2 teaspoons salt
1½ tablespoons pepper
8 skinned and boned chicken breasts
12 (6-inch) flour tortillas
1 avocado, peeled and sliced
2 cups (8 ounces) shredded Monterey Jack cheese
1 red bell pepper, cut into strips
1 yellow bell pepper, cut into strips
6 romaine lettuce leaves
Sour cream
Salsa

WHISK together first 6 ingredients in a shallow dish or large zip-top freezer bag; add chicken. Cover or seal, and chill 1 to 2 hours, turning occasionally.

REMOVE chicken from marinade, discarding marinade.

GRILL, covered with grill lid, over medium-high heat (350° to 400°) 20

to 25 minutes or until done. Chop 4 chicken breasts (reserve remaining chicken for Quick Chicken Tostadas on page 67). Top tortillas evenly with chicken, avocado, and next 4 ingredients; roll up, and serve with sour cream and salsa.

Cheesy Tomato Pie

MAKES 8 SERVINGS
PREP: 20 MIN., BAKE: 1 HR.

Round out the meal with fresh sliced melon, a bowlful of berries, and tangy lemonade.

½ (15-ounce) package refrigerated piecrusts
1 small red bell pepper, chopped
½ red onion, chopped
2 garlic cloves, minced
2 tablespoons olive oil
2 tablespoons chopped fresh basil
4 large eggs
1 cup half-and-half
1 teaspoon salt
½ teaspoon pepper
2 cups (8 ounces) shredded Monterey Jack cheese
⅓ cup shredded Parmesan cheese
3 plum tomatoes, cut into ¼-inch-thick slices

Beef Salad Niçoise

MAKES 6 TO 8 SERVINGS
PREP: 25 MIN.

Serve this hearty salad with crusty baguettes and red wine or sparkling water. Look for niçoise olives at specialty stores and kalamata olives in the ethnic foods section of the supermarket.

1 pound fresh green beans, trimmed
6 small new potatoes, cut in half
1 grilled flank steak (recipe, page 65)
9 to 12 cups gourmet mixed greens
2 red onions, halved and sliced
12 plum tomatoes, quartered
¾ cup niçoise or kalamata olives
1 (8-ounce) bottle balsamic vinaigrette or Ranch dressing

COOK green beans in boiling water in a saucepan 5 minutes or until crisp-tender; drain. Plunge into ice water to stop the cooking process; drain and set aside.

COOK potatoes in boiling water to cover in saucepan 15 minutes or until tender; drain and cool slightly. Cut into quarters.

CUT flank steak diagonally across the grain into thin strips.

MOUND steak strips in center of a lettuce-lined platter. Arrange green beans, potato, onion, tomato, and olives around flank steak. Serve with balsamic vinaigrette or Ranch dressing.

Quick Chicken Tostadas

MAKES 6 SERVINGS
PREP: 15 MIN., BAKE: 9 MIN.

Accompany these tostadas with orange wedges and salsa-spiked refried beans.

6 (6-inch) flour tortillas
2 tablespoons butter, melted
4 grilled chicken breasts, chopped
   (fajita recipe, facing page)
2 tomatoes, chopped
1 (4.5-ounce) can chopped green chiles
½ cup (2 ounces) shredded Monterey Jack
   cheese
½ cup (2 ounces) shredded Cheddar cheese
3 green onions, chopped
Paprika (optional)
Sour cream

PLACE tortillas in a single layer on baking sheets; brush with butter.
BAKE at 400° for 4 to 5 minutes or until lightly browned.
COMBINE chicken, tomato, and chiles; spoon evenly onto tortillas. Top evenly with cheeses and green onions; sprinkle with paprika, if desired. Bake 3 to 4 more minutes or until cheeses melt. Serve with sour cream.

Ingredients List

Here's a list of ingredients you'll need to prepare all the recipes.

To Pack from Your Pantry
- ❏ 4 teaspoons granulated sugar
- ❏ 6 tablespoons olive oil
- ❏ 1 cup vegetable oil
- ❏ salt, pepper
- ❏ 2½ tablespoons cracked pepper
- ❏ 9 garlic cloves
- ❏ ⅔ cup dry white wine
- ❏ paprika

From the Produce Stand
- ❏ 3 limes
- ❏ 17 plum tomatoes
- ❏ 2 tomatoes
- ❏ 3 green onions
- ❏ 1 pound fresh green beans
- ❏ 6 small new potatoes
- ❏ 3 red onions
- ❏ 1 bunch romaine lettuce
- ❏ 9 to 12 cups gourmet mixed
   greens
- ❏ 3 yellow bell peppers
- ❏ 4 red bell peppers
- ❏ 1 avocado

A Trip to the Market
- ❏ 2 (1½-pound) flank steaks
- ❏ 8 skinned and boned chicken breasts
- ❏ 1 (16-ounce) French bread loaf
- ❏ 18 (6-inch) flour tortillas
- ❏ ½ (15-ounce) package refrigerated
   piecrusts
- ❏ 1 (8-ounce) bottle balsamic
   vinaigrette or Ranch dressing
- ❏ 1 (8-ounce) jar salsa
- ❏ 1 (4.5-ounce) can chopped green
   chiles
- ❏ ¾ cup niçoise or kalamata olives
- ❏ 1 bunch fresh cilantro
- ❏ 1 bunch fresh basil
- ❏ ⅔ cup shredded Parmesan cheese
- ❏ 4½ cups (18 ounces) shredded
   Monterey Jack cheese
- ❏ ½ cup (2 ounces) shredded
   Cheddar cheese
- ❏ 1 (8-ounce) container soft
   cream cheese
- ❏ 4 large eggs
- ❏ 1 cup half-and-half
- ❏ 1 (16-ounce) container sour cream
- ❏ 2 tablespoons butter

Garden Fiesta

Serves 8

Rio Grande Limeade

Roasted Poblano Chile
con Queso

Adobo Grilled Pork Tacos With
Cucumber-Radish Salsa

Grilled Chicken Tortas

Margarita-Key Lime Pie With
Gingersnap Crust

Fiesta in El Paso

*Park Kerr specializes in Southwestern flavors,
and his favorite place to entertain is his patio.*

Park Kerr's perpetual search for interesting salsas, exotic chiles, and spicy condiments keeps him circling the globe. He began his El Paso Chile Company, a thriving retail business, in 1980 by selling strings of dried chiles on street corners in El Paso. His passion for chiles—from smoky chipotles to mild Anaheims—fuels the selection of salsas and hot stuff his company offers.

This true love of bold flavors surfaces in his cooking and entertaining. A favorite gathering spot is his walled Mexican garden. "My wife, Martina, gets all the credit for our lovely garden," says Park. "It's our oasis in a busy urban city. My natural position is tending the grill, with a big ol' margarita in my hand."

He uses a variety of peppers to deliver big flavors, not just scorching heat, that everyone can enjoy. "When I entertain, it's casual fun, friends in the yard, and all hands on deck," Park says, "and the kids are always included."

Autumn presents him with two reasons to celebrate: the pepper harvest and glorious weather. So bring the Southwest to your own backyard with a few of Park's favorite recipes.

(left) Rio Grande Limeade, Roasted Poblano Chile con Queso, and Adobo Grilled Pork Tacos With Cucumber-Radish Salsa. (above center) Park cools off with a glass of his Rio Grande Limeade.

"When I entertain, it's casual fun, friends in the yard, and all hands on deck," Park says, "and the kids are always included."

Rio Grande Limeade

MAKES 3 QUARTS
PREP: 10 MIN., CHILL: 8 HRS.

2 (12-ounce) cans frozen limeade
  concentrate, thawed and undiluted
3 cups tequila
3 cups water
2 cups orange liqueur
1 cup fresh lime juice
Garnish: lime slices

STIR together first 5 ingredients. Chill 8 hours. Serve over ice, and garnish, if desired.

Roasted Poblano Chile con Queso

MAKES 3½ CUPS
PREP: 20 MIN., GRILL: 7 MIN., STAND: 10 MIN.,
COOK: 10 MIN.

Add two pureed chipotle peppers in adobo sauce for heat and a smoky flavor.

3 poblano chile peppers
2 red Anaheim chile peppers
1 large onion, minced
2 garlic cloves, minced
2 tablespoons olive oil
2 cups (8 ounces) shredded Monterey Jack
  cheese
1 (8-ounce) loaf pasteurized prepared cheese
  product, cubed
½ cup half-and-half
Tortilla chips
Garnish: chopped red Anaheim chile peppers

GRILL poblano and 2 Anaheim peppers, without grill lid, over medium-high heat (350° to 400°) 5 to 7 minutes or until peppers look blistered, turning often.
PLACE peppers in a zip-top freezer bag; seal and let stand 10 minutes to loosen skins. Peel peppers; discard seeds. Slice peppers into thin strips.
SAUTÉ onion and garlic in hot oil in a large skillet over medium-high heat. Add peppers, and cook 2 minutes or until tender; reduce heat to low. Add cheeses and half-and-half, stirring until cheese melts. Serve warm with tortilla chips. Garnish, if desired.
NOTE: For testing purposes only, we used Velveeta for the cheese product.

Adobo Grilled Pork Tacos With Cucumber-Radish Salsa get their bold flavor from New Mexico chiles, cumin, and garlic.

Make-Ahead Hints

This intensely flavored menu is definitely worth the time, and much of it can be done ahead.

Two days before:
- Make Rio Grande Limeade; chill.

The day before:
- Grill, peel, and slice peppers for the queso and tortas; refrigerate in a zip-top plastic bag.
- Make Margarita-Key Lime Pie With Gingersnap Crust; cover and freeze.
- Make Cucumber-Radish Salsa; cover and chill.
- Shred and cube cheeses for queso and tortas; refrigerate in zip-top plastic bags.
- Prepare marinade for Adobo Grilled Pork Tacos.
- Flatten chicken breasts; chill in zip-top plastic bags.

That day:
- Prepare Roasted Poblano Chile con Queso; keep warm in a slow cooker or fondue pot.
- Marinate and grill pork; warm tortillas.
- Marinate and grill chicken; assemble tortas.
- Remove pie from freezer 40 minutes before serving.

Adobo Grilled Pork Tacos With Cucumber-Radish Salsa

MAKES 24 SERVINGS
PREP: 15 MIN., STAND: 30 MIN.,
CHILL: 30 MIN., GRILL: 20 MIN.

1 (2-ounce) package dried mild New Mexico chiles
2 teaspoons cumin seeds
1 tablespoon dried oregano
3 garlic cloves
2 tablespoons cider vinegar
1 teaspoon sugar
¼ teaspoon salt
¼ teaspoon ground red pepper
2 (¾-pound) pork tenderloins
1 (8-ounce) container sour cream
Cucumber-Radish Salsa
24 corn or flour tortillas, warmed
Garnishes: lime wedges, fresh cilantro

SLICE dried chiles in half lengthwise. Remove and discard stems and seeds. Place chiles in a bowl, and add boiling water to cover. Let stand 20 minutes or until chiles are softened. Drain chiles, reserving liquid.

COOK cumin seeds in a skillet over medium heat 30 seconds. Add oregano, and cook, stirring constantly, 30 seconds or until cumin is toasted.

PROCESS cumin mixture, soaked chiles, 1 cup reserved liquid, garlic, and next 4 ingredients in a blender or food processor until smooth, adding more reserved liquid if needed.

PLACE pork in a shallow dish or zip-top freezer bag. Pour half of chile mixture over meat. Cover or seal, and chill 30 minutes. Remove pork from marinade, discarding marinade.

STIR together sour cream and ½ cup Cucumber-Radish Salsa; cover and chill until ready to serve.

GRILL pork, covered with grill lid, over medium-high heat (350° to 400°), turning occasionally and basting with reserved chile mixture, 20 minutes or until a meat thermometer inserted into thickest portion registers 155°.

REMOVE from grill; let stand 10 minutes until pork reaches 160°. Coarsely chop pork. Serve in warm tortillas with remaining Cucumber-Radish Salsa and sour cream mixture. Garnish, if desired.

Cucumber-Radish Salsa:

MAKES 3 CUPS
PREP: 10 MIN.

2 cucumbers, peeled, seeded, and chopped
1 (6-ounce) package radishes, grated
1 small onion, minced
2 tablespoons chopped fresh cilantro
¼ cup lime juice
½ teaspoon salt
¼ teaspoon ground red pepper
Garnish: whole radish

STIR together first 7 ingredients. Cover and chill, if desired. Garnish, if desired.

Grilled Chicken Tortas

MAKES 8 SERVINGS
PREP: 35 MIN., CHILL: 1 HR., STAND: 10 MIN.,
GRILL: 17 MIN.

4 large skinned and boned chicken breasts
1 (16-ounce) container refrigerated hot chile salsa
¼ cup tequila
2 tablespoons chopped fresh cilantro
2 tablespoons lime juice
3 poblano chile peppers
¼ teaspoon salt
1 (16-ounce) can refried beans or black beans
1 tablespoon olive oil
8 (6-inch) crusty sandwich rolls, split
3 avocados, peeled and mashed
2 cups (8 ounces) shredded Monterey Jack cheese

PLACE chicken breasts between 2 sheets of heavy-duty plastic wrap, and flatten to a ¼-inch thickness using a meat mallet or rolling pin.

STIR together salsa and next 3 ingredients. Remove 1 cup mixture, and reserve; set aside remaining mixture.

PLACE chicken in a shallow dish or zip-top freezer bag; pour 1 cup reserved salsa mixture over chicken. Cover or seal; chill 1 hour, turning occasionally. Remove chicken from marinade; discard marinade.

GRILL peppers, covered with grill lid, over medium-high heat (350° to 400°) 5 to 7 minutes, turning often, until peppers look blistered.

PLACE peppers in a zip-top freezer bag; seal and let stand 10 minutes to loosen skins. Peel peppers; remove and discard seeds. Cut peppers into thin strips; set aside.

GRILL chicken, covered with grill lid, over medium-high heat (350° to 400°) about 5 minutes on each side or until done. Cool slightly. Cut chicken into thin slices, and sprinkle evenly with salt.

STIR together beans and olive oil in a 1-quart glass bowl, and microwave at HIGH 2 minutes or until thoroughly heated, stirring once.

SPREAD beans evenly over bottom halves of rolls. Spread avocado over top halves of rolls. Top bottom halves evenly with chicken, pepper strips, cheese, and top halves of rolls. Serve with remaining salsa mixture.

Margarita-Key Lime Pie With Gingersnap Crust

MAKES 1 (9-INCH) PIE
PREP: 25 MIN., COOL: 2 HRS., FREEZE: 2 HRS.,
STAND: 20 MIN.

4 large eggs
½ cup fresh Key lime juice
¼ cup orange liqueur
¼ cup tequila
2 (14-ounce) cans sweetened condensed milk
2 teaspoons grated lime rind
2 cups whipping cream
Gingersnap Crust
Garnishes: lime rind curls, sweetened whipped cream

COMBINE first 5 ingredients in a heavy saucepan over medium heat, stirring often, 20 minutes or until a candy thermometer registers 165°; remove from heat. Stir in lime rind; cool 2 hours or until completely cooled.

BEAT whipping cream at high speed with an electric mixer until soft peaks form. Fold into egg mixture. Spoon into Gingersnap Crust.

FREEZE 2 hours or until firm. Let stand 20 minutes before cutting. Garnish, if desired.

Gingersnap Crust:

MAKES 1 (9-INCH) CRUST
PREP: 15 MIN., BAKE: 8 MIN.

¾ cup sweetened flaked coconut, toasted
18 gingersnap cookies, crumbled
3 tablespoons unsalted butter, melted

STIR together all ingredients. Press into bottom and up sides of a 9-inch pieplate.

BAKE at 350° for 8 minutes. Cool on a wire rack.

Tequila and orange liqueur add punch to Margarita-Key Lime Pie With Gingersnap Crust.

Italian Goes Light

You can serve your guests this great meal without guilt.

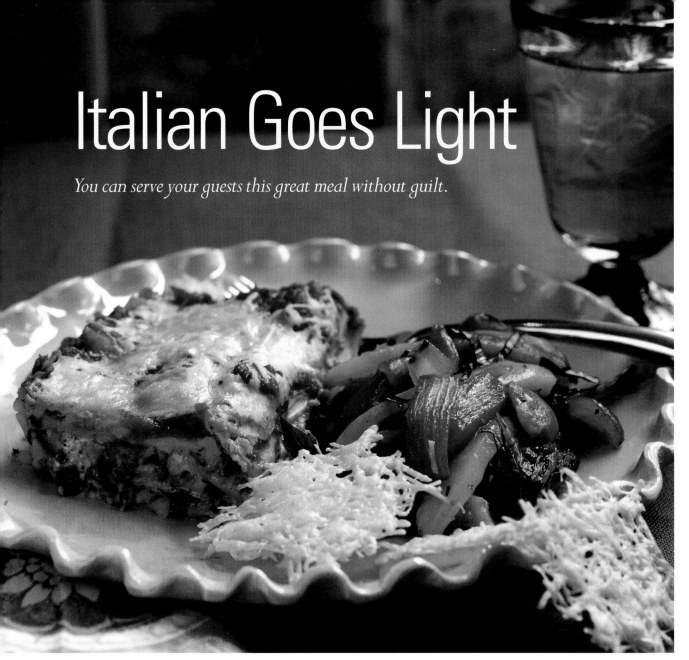

Only the flavor is rich in Cheesy Spinach Lasagna, Roasted Tomato-and-Pepper Salad, and Parmesan Crisps.

Italian dishes are often reserved for special-occasion calorie splurges. But you can easily replace high-fat meats with leaner cuts and vegetables such as mushrooms. Vegetables such as spinach, zucchini, and carrots add a fiber-rich boost of flavor to classics like lasagna.

If you must have meat, try our Cheesy Spinach Lasagna with Canadian bacon, which is naturally low in fat. These recipes show that Italian dishes can be health foods as well as comfort foods when packed with nutritious ingredients.

Parmesan Crisps

MAKES 2 DOZEN
PREP: 15 MIN., BAKE: 8 MIN.

Cookie cutters make useful molds for these light and easy wafers.

Vegetable cooking spray
1½ cups (6 ounces) finely shredded
   Parmesan cheese

COAT the inside of a 2-inch cookie cutter with cooking spray, and place on an aluminum-foil lined baking sheet coated with cooking spray. Sprinkle 1 tablespoon cheese inside the cutter, and remove cutter; repeat with remaining cheese, leaving 1 inch between rounds.

BAKE at 350° for 8 minutes or until lightly browned. Quickly remove cheese wafers from baking sheet with a spatula. Cool on a wire rack. Store in an airtight container.

PER 2 CRISPS: CALORIES 118 (59% FROM FAT); FAT 7.7G (SAT 5G, MONO 2.5G, POLY 0.2G); PROTEIN 11G; CARB 1G; FIBER 0G; CHOL 21MG; IRON 0.3MG; SODIUM 481MG; CALC 355MG

Roasted Tomato-and-Pepper Salad

MAKES 6 SERVINGS
PREP: 15 MIN., BROIL: 30 MIN., STAND: 10 MIN.

6 large plum tomatoes
Vegetable cooking spray
1 yellow bell pepper
1 green bell pepper
1 red bell pepper
1 medium-size red onion, cut into eighths
1 tablespoon olive oil
1 tablespoon balsamic vinegar
1 garlic clove, minced
½ teaspoon salt
½ teaspoon dried oregano
½ teaspoon freshly ground pepper
¼ cup sliced fresh basil

CUT tomatoes into ¼-inch-thick slices.
ARRANGE on an aluminum foil-lined baking sheet coated with cooking spray.
BROIL, 5 inches from heat, 5 minutes on each side; set tomato aside.
CUT bell peppers in half lengthwise; remove and discard seeds.
ARRANGE peppers, cut sides down, and onion on a foil-lined baking sheet coated with cooking spray.
BROIL, 5 inches from heat, 8 to 10 minutes on each side or until peppers look blistered. Remove peppers, and broil onion pieces 3 more minutes, if necessary.
PLACE peppers in a zip-top plastic bag; seal and let stand 10 minutes to loosen skins. Peel peppers; cut into thin strips.
WHISK together oil and next 5 ingredients in a large bowl; add vegetables, tossing to coat. Sprinkle with basil.

PER SERVING: CALORIES 61 (38% FROM FAT);
FAT 2.6G (SAT 0.4G, MONO 1.8G, POLY 0.3G);
PROTEIN 1.4G; CARB 9G; FIBER 2.3G; CHOL 0MG;
IRON 0.8MG; SODIUM 201MG; CALC 28MG

Cheesy Spinach Lasagna

MAKES 8 SERVINGS
PREP: 20 MIN., BAKE: 35 MIN., STAND: 5 MIN.

To reduce sodium, omit the Canadian bacon and salt.

9 uncooked lasagna noodles
2 cups (8 ounces) shredded part-skim mozzarella cheese, divided
1 (16-ounce) container fat-free ricotta cheese
1 (10-ounce) package frozen chopped spinach, thawed and well drained
½ cup freshly grated Parmesan cheese
1 teaspoon dried Italian seasoning
½ teaspoon garlic powder
¼ teaspoon salt
1 (3-ounce) package Canadian bacon, chopped
½ small onion, diced
Vegetable cooking spray
1 (26-ounce) jar low-fat pasta sauce

COOK pasta according to package directions; set aside.
STIR together 1½ cups mozzarella cheese and next 6 ingredients.
SAUTÉ chopped Canadian bacon and onion in a skillet coated with cooking spray over medium heat 5 to 6 minutes or until onion is tender. Stir into cheese mixture.
SPREAD ½ cup pasta sauce in an 11- x 7-inch baking dish coated with cooking spray. Layer with 3 noodles and ½ cup pasta sauce; top with half of cheese mixture. Repeat layers once, ending with remaining cheese mixture. Top with remaining 3 noodles and remaining pasta sauce.
BAKE at 350° for 30 minutes. Sprinkle with remaining ½ cup mozzarella cheese; bake 5 more minutes or until cheese melts. Let stand 5 minutes.
NOTE: Freeze individual portions as desired. To reheat, bake, covered, at 300° for 1 hour.

PER SERVING: CALORIES 295 (22% FROM FAT);
FAT 7.3G (SAT 4.3G, MONO 2.2G, POLY 0.5G);
PROTEIN 24G; CARB 33G; FIBER 3.6G; CHOL 42MG;
IRON 2.9MG; SODIUM 799MG; CALC 504MG

Two-Layered Ice-Cream Freeze

MAKES 8 SERVINGS
PREP: 30 MIN.; FREEZE: 3 HRS., 30 MIN.

2 cups no-sugar-added, fat-free vanilla ice cream, softened
1 (16-ounce) container fat-free frozen whipped topping, thawed and divided
1 teaspoon almond extract
10 store-bought meringue cookies, crushed
2 cups no-sugar-added fat-free chocolate fudge ice cream, softened
1½ cups fresh or frozen raspberries, thawed
¼ cup sugar
1 tablespoon lemon juice

STIR together vanilla ice cream, ½ cup whipped topping, and almond extract. Spoon mixture into a plastic wrap-lined 2-quart glass bowl, and freeze 15 minutes or until set.
STIR together 1½ cups whipped topping and cookie crumbs; spread evenly over vanilla ice-cream mixture, and freeze 15 minutes.
STIR together chocolate fudge ice cream and ½ cup whipped topping. Spread over cookie crumb mixture. Cover and freeze 3 hours or until firm.
PROCESS raspberries in a blender or food processor until smooth. Pour through a fine wire-mesh strainer into a small saucepan, pressing pulp with back of a wooden spoon; discard seeds. Bring raspberry puree, sugar, and lemon juice to a boil, stirring constantly; cook, stirring constantly, 2 minutes or until thickened.
REMOVE ice-cream mixture from freezer. Dip glass bowl in warm water 15 seconds. Invert onto a serving dish, discarding plastic wrap. Cut ice cream into wedges; serve with raspberry sauce and, if desired, remaining whipped topping.

PER SERVING: CALORIES 261 (0% FROM FAT);
FAT 0G; PROTEIN 4.2G; CARB 57G; FIBER 2G;
CHOL 0MG; IRON 0.3MG; SODIUM 130MG; CALC 66MG

Goblins Are Gathering

We've assembled all the fixin's for a "spooktacular" party.

The chills and thrills of Halloween bring family and friends together to share the spooky spirit with creative costumes and whimsical touches.

Make your gathering easy by keeping the decorations and food simple. Explore the fall foliage, and let it set the tone with bales of hay and cornstalks. Get everyone in the mood with a few games, and let the child in you shine through dunking for apples and sharing ghost tales.

Goblin Dip With Bone Crackers

MAKES 6 CUPS
PREP: 10 MIN., COOK: 15 MIN.

1 (16-ounce) can chili without beans
1 (16-ounce) can refried beans
1 (8-ounce) package cream cheese
1 (8-ounce) jar chunky pico de gallo
1 (4.5-ounce) can chopped green chiles, undrained
½ teaspoon ground cumin
Toppings: shredded Cheddar or Monterey Jack cheese with peppers, chopped black olives, sliced green onions
Bone Crackers

COOK first 6 ingredients in a heavy saucepan over low heat, stirring often, 15 minutes or until cream cheese is melted. Sprinkle with desired toppings, and serve warm with Bone Crackers.

Bone Crackers:
MAKES 60 CRACKERS
PREP: 20 MIN., BAKE: 30 MIN.

2 (13.5-ounce) packages 9-inch flour tortillas
½ cup butter or margarine, melted
¼ teaspoon garlic salt

CUT tortillas with a 3½-inch bone-shaped cutter, and place on baking sheets. Stir together butter and garlic salt; brush mixture on cutouts.

Your guests will love the bold Southwest flavor of Goblin Dip With Bone Crackers.

BAKE at 250° for 30 minutes or until crisp.
NOTE: Flour tortillas can be cut into bone shapes using kitchen shears.

Jack-o'-Lantern Cheeseburger Pie

MAKES 6 TO 8 SERVINGS
PREP: 30 MIN., BAKE: 30 MIN.

1 pound ground beef
1 medium onion, chopped
2 garlic cloves, pressed
¾ teaspoon salt
½ teaspoon pepper
¼ cup ketchup
1 teaspoon Worcestershire sauce
1 (15-ounce) package refrigerated piecrusts
1 tablespoon prepared mustard
3 cups (12 ounces) shredded Monterey Jack cheese, divided
2 tablespoons water
1 large egg
Red and yellow liquid food coloring

COOK first 5 ingredients in a large skillet over medium-high heat, stirring until beef crumbles and is no longer pink; drain. Stir in ketchup and Worcestershire sauce; cool.

UNFOLD 1 piecrust, and place on a lightly greased baking sheet. Spread mustard evenly over crust. Stir together meat mixture and 2 cups cheese; spoon onto center of crust, leaving a 2-inch border.

UNFOLD remaining piecrust, and cut out a jack-o'-lantern face, reserving pastry cutouts to use as a stem. Place crust over meat mixture; fold edges under, and crimp. Place stem on top of jack-o'-lantern face.

WHISK together 2 tablespoons water, egg, and 1 drop each of red and yellow food coloring; brush over crust. **BAKE** at 425° for 20 minutes; remove from oven, and brush again with egg mixture. Fill eyes, nose, and mouth with remaining 1 cup cheese. Bake 5 to 10 more minutes or until golden brown.

Cheesy Witches' Brooms

MAKES 16 SERVINGS
PREP: 15 MIN., BAKE: 12 MIN.

2 (11-ounce) packages cornbread twists or
   breadsticks
½ cup shredded Parmesan cheese

SEPARATE cornbread twists, and place on an ungreased baking sheet. Flatten 1 end of dough, and cut dough into small strips to resemble a broom. Sprinkle cut end with cheese.

BAKE brooms at 375° for 10 to 12 minutes or until lightly browned.

Bat Sandwiches

MAKES 24 SANDWICHES
PREP: 30 MIN.

3 cups (12 ounces) shredded sharp Cheddar
   cheese
1 (8-ounce) container chive-and-onion cream
   cheese, softened
1 (4-ounce) jar diced pimiento, drained
½ cup chopped pecans, toasted
24 whole wheat or pumpernickel bread
   slices

STIR together first 4 ingredients. Using a 3- to 4-inch bat-shaped cutter, cut 2 bats from each bread slice. Spread about 2 tablespoons filling over 24 bats. Top with remaining 24 bats.

Witches' Brew Chicken Soup

MAKES 12 CUPS
PREP: 15 MIN., COOK: 40 MIN.

1 tablespoon butter or margarine
4 skinned and boned chicken breasts,
   chopped
1 large onion, chopped
3 carrots, chopped
2 garlic cloves, minced
2 (14-ounce) cans low-sodium chicken broth
1 tablespoon chicken bouillon granules
1 teaspoon ground cumin
¼ teaspoon ground red pepper
3 (16-ounce) cans great Northern beans,
   rinsed, drained, and divided
1 (4.5-ounce) can chopped green chiles
2 tablespoons all-purpose flour
½ cup milk
¼ cup chopped fresh cilantro
Toppings: shredded Cheddar cheese, sour
   cream, sliced green onions, cooked and
   crumbled bacon

Scare up a devilishly good time with Witches' Brew Chicken Soup and Cheesy Witches' Brooms.

MELT butter in a large Dutch oven over medium-high heat; add chicken and next 3 ingredients, and sauté 10 minutes. Stir in broth and next 3 ingredients.

BRING to a boil; reduce heat, and simmer, stirring occasionally, 20 minutes. Stir in 2 cans beans and green chiles.

MASH remaining beans in a small bowl. Whisk together flour and milk, and stir into beans. Gradually add bean mixture to soup mixture, stirring constantly. Cook 10 minutes or until thickened. Remove from heat, and stir in cilantro. Serve with desired toppings.

A basket of fall's bounty adds festive color to your gathering.

Trash Mix

MAKES 16 CUPS
PREP: 5 MIN.

1 (16-ounce) package candy corn
1 (15-ounce) package pretzel nibblers
1 (12-ounce) package caramel popcorn and
  peanuts
1 (15-ounce) package banana chips
1 (15-ounce) package candy-coated
  chocolate pieces
1 (15-ounce) package dried mango
1 (15-ounce) package dried pineapple
1 (10-ounce) package toffee pretzels
1 (6-ounce) package sweetened dried
  cranberries
1 (6-ounce) package worm-shaped chewy
  candy

STIR together all ingredients. Store in an airtight container.

NOTE: For testing purposes only, we used Crunch 'n Munch, pretzel Nuggets, M&M's, and Craisins.

Party Perfect

■ **Choose** a party theme. Plan your menu, and make a checklist. Getting organized is the key to successful entertaining.
■ **Etch** or print handmade invitations on construction paper or handmade papers.
■ **Light** the inside of carved pumpkins and gourds with candles, or use cordless battery-powered candles. Gourds that haven't been carved completely through can provide muted light.
■ **Embellish** the driveway, walkway, windowsills, door knockers, lamppost, and porch fronts with odd-sized pumpkins, vines, and green and white gourds.
■ **Attach** natural swags or vines to the backs of chairs with twine. The backs of chairs can be as fun as the table decorations.
■ **Round** up flashlights and camping lanterns for folks to use in the dark. Tape a spooky stencil over the bulb of a flashlight to create mysterious shadows.
■ **Have** one or two large arrangements greet guests as they arrive. Include fall produce, gourds, nuts, mums, and dried leaves around the base of the arrangement. Cast-iron kettles make creative floral pots.
■ **Transform** a garage, loft, or recreation room into a barn setting.
■ **Enjoy** your company. When you relax, your guests will, too.

Filled with everything from caramel popcorn to candy corn, Trash Mix is a hit with kids and adults.

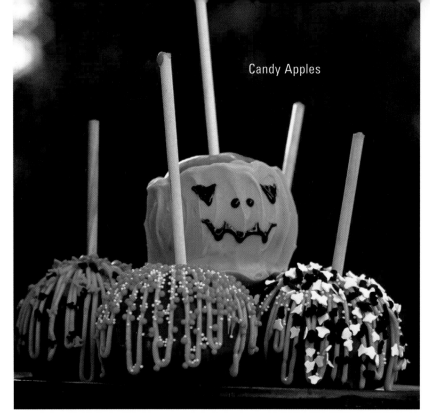

Candy Apples

Ghosts on a Stick

MAKES 2 DOZEN
PREP: 25 MIN., CHILL: 1 HR., BAKE: 10 MIN.

½ cup butter or margarine, softened
½ cup shortening
1½ cups powdered sugar
1 large egg
2 teaspoons vanilla extract
2¾ cups all-purpose flour
1 teaspoon cream of tartar
½ teaspoon baking soda
Wooden craft sticks
1 (16-ounce) container ready-to-spread
    vanilla frosting
Toppings: colored sugars, mini-morsels,
    candy sprinkles, 1 (4.25-ounce) tube black
    or brown decorating frosting

BEAT butter and shortening at medium speed with an electric mixer until blended. Add powdered sugar, egg, and vanilla to butter mixture; beat well. Gradually add flour, cream of tartar, and baking soda, beating well.

COVER and chill dough 1 hour. Roll dough to ¼-inch thickness, and cut with a 4-inch ghost-shaped cutter. Place cookies 2 inches apart on lightly greased baking sheets. Place a craft stick under each cookie, pressing cookie lightly onto stick.

BAKE at 375° for 10 minutes or until cookies are lightly browned. Cool

Candy Apples

MAKES 8 APPLES
PREP: 40 MIN.

8 wooden craft sticks
8 medium Gala apples
2 (6.5-ounce) packages caramel apple wraps
1 (16-ounce) milk chocolate bar
16 ounces vanilla bark coating
Orange paste food coloring
Toppings: colored sprinkles, chopped
    peanuts, black writing gel

INSERT craft sticks into apples. Cover each apple with 1 caramel wrap.

MICROWAVE at HIGH 15 to 20 seconds. Cool on wax paper.

MELT chocolate bar in a small saucepan over low heat.

DIP each apple into chocolate; let dry on wax paper.

MELT vanilla bark coating in a small saucepan over low heat; stir in orange food coloring. Dip or drizzle each apple with vanilla coating mixture. Decorate with desired toppings, and let dry on wax paper.

NOTE: For testing purposes only, we used Ghirardelli Milk Chocolate baking bar.

Shrunken Heads

MAKES: 8 HEADS
PREP: 45 MIN., STAND: 1 WEEK

8 small Granny Smith apples, peeled
1 cup lemon juice
1 tablespoon salt
Red licorice, cut into short lengths

CORE apples, and carve face features.

COMBINE lemon juice and salt. Add apples; toss to coat. Let stand 1 minute. Drain; let stand at room temperature 1 week. Add licorice for hair.

Shrunken Heads

Everyone will quickly forget Halloween tricks when they see the spread of ghoulish good treats.

cookies on baking sheets 5 minutes, and remove to wire racks to cool completely.

MICROWAVE frosting in a 2-quart glass bowl at HIGH 1 minute or until frosting melts. Spread melted frosting over cookies in batches of 3. (Frosting hardens quickly.) Decorate rapidly with desired toppings.

Candy Corn Chocolate Cakes

MAKES 16 SERVINGS
PREP: 40 MIN., BAKE: 40 MIN., FREEZE: 30 MIN.

2 cups sugar
2 cups all-purpose flour
1 cup unsweetened cocoa
1 cup vegetable oil
1 teaspoon salt
2 large eggs
1 cup buttermilk
1 cup hot water
2 teaspoons baking soda
2 teaspoons vanilla extract
Buttercream Frosting

BEAT first 6 ingredients in a large bowl at medium speed with an electric mixer until blended. Stir in buttermilk. **STIR** together 1 cup hot water and baking soda; stir into batter. Stir in

vanilla. Pour into 2 greased and floured 9-inch round cakepans.
BAKE at 350° for 30 to 40 minutes or until a wooden pick inserted in center comes out clean. Cool in pans on wire racks 10 minutes; remove from pans, and cool completely on wire racks.
FREEZE layers 30 minutes. Cut each layer into 8 wedges.
PIPE Buttercream Frosting on top and sides of cake wedges to resemble candy corn. Using a medium star tip, pipe white frosting on the small end of each cake, yellow frosting on center, and orange on wide end.

Buttercream Frosting:

MAKES 3½ CUPS
PREP: 10 MIN.

1 cup butter or margarine, softened
1 (2-pound) package powdered sugar
⅓ cup milk
1 teaspoon vanilla extract
Orange food coloring paste
Yellow food coloring paste

BEAT butter at medium speed with an electric mixer until fluffy; gradually add powdered sugar, and beat until light and fluffy. Add milk, beating until spreading consistency. Stir in vanilla.
STIR desired amount of orange food

coloring into 1½ cups frosting. Stir desired amount of yellow food coloring into 1¼ cups frosting.

Fudgy Hot Cocoa

MAKES 10 TO 12 SERVINGS
PREP: 10 MIN., COOK: 10 MIN.

10 cups milk
1 cup chocolate syrup
⅔ cup unsweetened cocoa
⅔ cup hot fudge topping
2 teaspoons vanilla extract
½ teaspoon almond extract
Sugar
24 large marshmallows
Black decorating frosting

COOK first 6 ingredients in a Dutch oven over medium-low heat, stirring occasionally, 10 minutes or until thoroughly heated. (Do not boil.)
SPRINKLE sugar onto wax paper; place marshmallows 2 inches apart on paper. Sprinkle marshmallows with sugar, and top with a sheet of wax paper. Flatten marshmallows with a rolling pin. Remove top sheet of wax paper, and cut marshmallows with Halloween cutters. Decorate with frosting, and serve in hot cocoa.

Fall means football, and what better way to enjoy pre- and post-game festivities than with a good old-fashioned tailgate party. These delicious and easy-to-prepare recipes include tasty updates on fried chicken, pasta salad, and the ever-popular Bloody Mary. Plus, with our tips below about traveling with food, you'll score points with the home team and visitors alike.

Take It on the Road

A gorgeous afternoon is the only excuse you need to load up your vehicle and head out with family and friends for a tailgate party. Use these handy tips for any outdoor meal.

■ Jars with tight-fitting lids make great containers for potato, pasta, and chicken salads.

■ If you don't have reusable ice packs, freeze bottles of water to keep foods cold. Later, the refreshing drinking water will be a bonus.

■ Carry a large, colorful disposable cloth for the table or a spot under a tree. For speedy cleanup, put all trash on the cloth and tie up the ends.

■ Be sure to include a heavy-duty zip-top freezer bag with insect repellent, sunscreen, cleansing wipes, and antibacterial hand sanitizer (for cleaning hands before preparing or serving food).

■ One hour is the maximum time food should be left unrefrigerated if the outside temperature is above 85 degrees. Pack your cooler directly from the refrigerator or freezer (placing foods to be kept the coolest on the bottom), and store with the lid sealed tight.

■ Remember to keep cooked and raw foods in separate containers (disposable containers work great). If you're going to be cooking, pack additional clean plates to avoid cross contamination of raw and cooked meats. Never put cooked food on a plate that previously held raw food. Also, make sure that meats are thawed completely before cooking and cooked to the proper temperature.

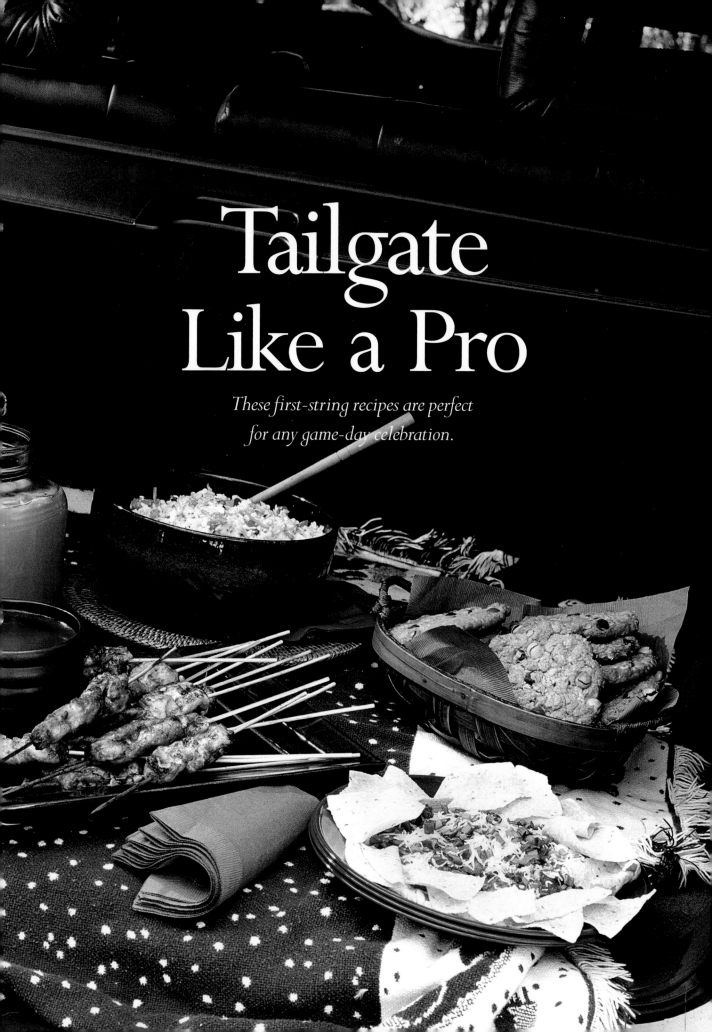

Tailgate Like a Pro

*These first-string recipes are perfect
for any game-day celebration.*

Green tea—an antioxidant that could reduce cancer risk—is the flavorful secret to Tailgate Punch.

STIR together first 7 ingredients in a pitcher; chill 1 hour. Stir in vodka, and pour into 6 glasses. Squeeze a lime wedge into each glass.

Tailgate Punch

MAKES 5 CUPS
PREP: 15 MIN., CHILL: 10 HRS.

¾ cup pineapple juice, divided
1 lemon, sliced
1 (5.5-ounce) can pineapple chunks, undrained
⅓ cup sugar
½ cup peach nectar
½ cup brewed green tea
2 cups ginger ale, chilled
1 cup sparkling water, chilled

COMBINE ½ cup pineapple juice and lemon slices in a zip-top freezer bag. Seal and chill 8 hours. Add pineapple chunks to freezer bag; seal and chill 2 hours. Place fruit mixture in a large pitcher.

STIR in remaining ¼ cup pineapple juice, sugar, peach nectar, and green tea until sugar dissolves. Add ginger ale and sparkling water; serve punch immediately.

NOTE: For testing purposes only, we used bottled Arizona green tea.

Bloody Mary

MAKES 4 CUPS
PREP: 10 MIN., CHILL: 1 HR.

2½ cups tomato juice
1½ tablespoons Worcestershire sauce
1 tablespoon lemon juice
1 tablespoon prepared horseradish
1 teaspoon celery salt
½ teaspoon pepper
½ teaspoon hot sauce
1 cup vodka
6 lime wedges

Pizza Dip

MAKES 4 APPETIZER SERVINGS
PREP: 15 MIN., BAKE 20 MIN.

1 (8-ounce) package light cream cheese, softened
½ cup light sour cream
¼ teaspoon garlic powder
¼ teaspoon dried oregano
¼ teaspoon ground red pepper
¾ cup pizza sauce
½ cup chopped pepperoni
3 green onions, chopped
1 cup (4 ounces) shredded mozzarella cheese
Tortilla chips

BEAT first 5 ingredients at medium speed with an electric mixer until blended. Spread evenly in a lightly greased 9-inch pieplate.

SPOON pizza sauce evenly over cream cheese mixture; sprinkle with pepperoni and green onions.

BAKE at 350° for 10 minutes. Sprinkle with mozzarella cheese, and bake 10 more minutes or until cheese melts. Serve with tortilla chips.

Mediterranean Pasta Salad

MAKES 8 TO 10 APPETIZER SERVINGS
PREP: 40 MIN., COOK: 14 MIN.

12 ounces uncooked orzo
2 tablespoons olive oil
1 large yellow bell pepper, seeded and diced
1 medium tomato, seeded and diced
1 small cucumber, seeded and diced
1 medium carrot, shredded
1 (8-ounce) package crumbled feta cheese
3 tablespoons pine nuts, toasted
2 to 3 tablespoons chopped fresh basil
2 tablespoons drained capers
½ cup olive oil
⅓ cup lemon juice
1 shallot, minced
6 garlic cloves, minced
2 teaspoons chopped fresh or 1 teaspoon dried mint
1 teaspoon ground cumin
1 teaspoon Dijon mustard
⅛ teaspoon salt
⅛ teaspoon pepper

COOK orzo according to package directions. Drain and rinse with cold water; drain again thoroughly.

STIR together orzo and 2 tablespoons olive oil in a large bowl. Stir in bell pepper and next 7 ingredients.

WHISK together ½ cup olive oil and next 8 ingredients. Pour over orzo mixture, and toss to coat.

Orzo forms the base for colorful Mediterranean Pasta Salad.

Most Valuable Cookies are a winning combination of oats, peanut butter, and chocolate.

Fried Chicken on a Stick

MAKES 12 APPETIZER SERVINGS
PREP: 25 MIN., CHILL: 8 HRS., COOK 35 MIN.

6 skinned and boned chicken breasts
Wooden skewers
1 cup buttermilk
1½ tablespoons Creole seasoning, divided
2 tablespoons coarse-grained mustard
½ teaspoon salt
⅛ teaspoon ground red pepper
2 cups all-purpose flour
Vegetable oil
Barbecue sauce

CUT chicken into 24 strips; thread each strip onto a 10-inch wooden skewer, and place in a shallow dish.
COMBINE buttermilk, 1 tablespoon Creole seasoning, and next 3 ingredients; pour over chicken. Cover and chill 8 hours, turning occasionally.
REMOVE chicken skewers from marinade, discarding marinade.
STIR together flour and remaining ½ tablespoon Creole seasoning. Dredge chicken skewers in flour mixture.
POUR oil to a depth of 1½ inches into a large, heavy skillet; heat to 350°. Fry chicken, in batches, 3 minutes on each side; drain on paper towels. Serve with barbecue sauce.

Fried Chicken on a Stick

Cream Cheese Rollups

MAKES 5 DOZEN APPETIZERS
PREP: 25 MIN., CHILL: 3 HRS.

2 (8-ounce) packages cream cheese, softened
1 (1-ounce) envelope Ranch dressing mix
4 green onions, chopped
1 (4.5-ounce) can chopped green chiles, drained
1 (4-ounce) jar diced pimiento, drained
⅓ cup chopped ripe olives
6 (8-inch) flour tortillas

BEAT cream cheese and Ranch dressing mix at medium speed with an electric mixer until fluffy. Stir in green onions and next 3 ingredients.
SPREAD cream cheese mixture evenly over tortillas; roll up. Wrap each in plastic wrap, and chill 3 hours. Cut each roll diagonally into 10 slices.

VEGETABLE ROLLUPS: Omit green chiles and pimiento. Stir in 1 celery rib, chopped; ½ cup chopped red bell pepper; and ½ cup chopped green bell pepper. Proceed as directed.
MEXICAN ROLLUPS: Omit 1 package cream cheese, dressing mix, green chiles, and pimiento. Stir in 2 cups (8 ounces) shredded sharp Cheddar cheese and 1 (4-ounce) can diced jalapeño peppers, drained. Proceed as directed. Serve with salsa.

Most Valuable Cookies

MAKES 2½ DOZEN
PREP: 35 MIN., BAKE: 15 MIN. PER BATCH

½ cup butter or margarine, softened
1 cup granulated sugar
1 cup plus 2 tablespoons firmly packed brown sugar
3 large eggs
2 cups creamy peanut butter
¼ teaspoon vanilla extract
4½ cups uncooked regular oats
2 teaspoons baking soda
¼ teaspoon salt
1 cup candy-coated chocolate pieces
1 cup semisweet chocolate morsels

BEAT butter at medium speed with an electric mixer until creamy; gradually add sugars, beating well. Add eggs, peanut butter, and vanilla, beating until blended.
STIR in oats, soda, and salt. (Dough will be stiff.) Stir in chocolate pieces and chocolate morsels.
PACK dough into a ¼-cup measure. Drop 4 inches apart onto lightly greased baking sheets. Lightly press each cookie into a 3½-inch circle.
BAKE at 350° for 12 to 15 minutes (cookie centers should be soft). Cool slightly on baking sheets; remove to wire racks, and let cool completely.
NOTE: For testing purposes only, we used M&M's for candy-coated chocolate pieces.

Luscious
Party Bites

Your guests will rave over these easy-to-make,
flavor-packed recipes.

Just because you're time-challenged doesn't mean you can't impress friends with a showstopping spread. These appetizers, most of which are very easy to prepare, will have everyone begging for the recipes as they make their second trip to the table. For those with a sweet tooth, we're including chocolaty, nutty Chewy Scotch Bars, page 87.

Tonight's Tasty Bites

Serves 8 to 10

Blue Cheese Terrine With
Tomato-Basil Vinaigrette

Spicy Party Meatballs

Chunky Black-Eyed Pea Salsa

Vegetable Platter With Creamy
Honey-Herb Dip

Smoked Salmon Canapés

Sesame-Maple Chicken Wings

Marinated Shrimp-and-
Artichokes

Chewy Scotch Bars

Take a shortcut with Marinated Shrimp-and-Artichokes, and buy steamed shrimp at your supermarket or seafood market. Blue Cheese Terrine With Tomato-Basil Vinaigrette looks and tastes spectacular.

Blue Cheese Terrine With Tomato-Basil Vinaigrette

MAKES 10 TO 12 APPETIZER SERVINGS
PREP: 30 MIN., BROIL: 10 MIN.,
STAND: 10 MIN., CHILL: 8 HRS.

For an hors d'oeuvre, serve this
top-rated terrine with toasted
French baguette slices.

2 red bell peppers, cut in half
2 yellow bell peppers, cut in half
6 ounces blue cheese, crumbled
2 (8-ounce) packages cream cheese, softened
Tomato-Basil Vinaigrette
Mixed salad greens

PLACE bell pepper halves, cut sides down, on an aluminum foil-lined baking sheet.
BROIL 5 inches from heat 8 to 10 minutes or until bell peppers look blistered.
PLACE bell peppers in a zip-top plastic bag; seal and let stand 10 minutes to loosen skins. Peel peppers; remove and discard seeds. Pat peppers dry with paper towels.
BEAT cheeses at medium speed with an electric mixer until smooth.
SPREAD half of cheese mixture in a plastic wrap-lined 8- x 4-inch loafpan. Top with 4 pepper halves. Spread remaining cheese mixture over peppers; top with remaining pepper halves. Cover and chill 8 hours.

UNMOLD onto a serving dish, and drizzle with Tomato-Basil Vinaigrette. Serve on mixed greens.

Tomato-Basil Vinaigrette:

MAKES 2 CUPS
PREP: 5 MIN.

¼ cup white wine vinegar
1 tablespoon Dijon mustard
1 teaspoon salt
½ teaspoon pepper
1 teaspoon lemon juice
½ cup olive oil
6 plum tomatoes, peeled, seeded, and diced
¼ cup chopped fresh basil

WHISK together first 5 ingredients in a small bowl. Gradually whisk in oil. Stir in tomato and basil.

Spicy Party Meatballs

MAKES 4 DOZEN
PREP: 5 MIN., COOK: 45 MIN.

1 (12-ounce) jar cocktail sauce
1 (10.5-ounce) jar jalapeño jelly
½ small sweet onion, minced
½ (3-pound) package frozen cooked
  meatballs

COOK first 3 ingredients in a Dutch oven over medium heat, stirring 5 minutes or until jelly melts and mixture is smooth.
STIR in meatballs. Reduce heat, and simmer, stirring occasionally, 35 to 40 minutes or until thoroughly heated.

Roasted poblano chile pepper adds a smoky, spicy zing to Chunky Black-Eyed Pea Salsa.

Chunky Black-Eyed Pea Salsa

MAKES 2 CUPS
PREP: 20 MIN., BROIL: 10 MIN., STAND: 10 MIN.

1 large poblano chile pepper
1 (15.8-ounce) can black-eyed peas, rinsed and drained
1 ripe mango, peeled and chopped
½ small sweet onion, chopped
½ small red bell pepper, chopped
¼ cup chopped fresh cilantro
½ teaspoon grated lime rind
3 tablespoons fresh lime juice
2 teaspoons olive oil
¼ to ½ teaspoon salt
¼ to ½ teaspoon black pepper
Tortilla chips

BROIL poblano pepper on an aluminum foil-lined baking sheet 5 inches from heat about 5 minutes on each side or until pepper looks blistered.
PLACE pepper in a zip-top plastic bag; seal and let stand 10 minutes to loosen skin. Peel pepper; remove and discard seeds. Chop pepper.

STIR together pepper, peas, and next 9 ingredients. Cover and chill. Serve with tortilla chips.

Vegetable Platter With Creamy Honey-Herb Dip

MAKES 8 SERVINGS
PREP: 15 MIN., COOK: 32 MIN.

To get a head start, wash lettuce, pat dry, and wrap in paper towels. Refrigerate in a zip-top plastic bag. Vegetables can be steamed 8 hours ahead and chilled.

6 new potatoes, halved
2 sweet potatoes, peeled and cubed (optional)
½ pound small fresh green beans, trimmed
2 cups fresh cauliflower florets
2 cups fresh broccoli florets
Lettuce leaves
Creamy Honey-Herb Dip

ARRANGE new potato and, if desired, sweet potato in a steamer basket over boiling water. Cover and steam 20 minutes or until tender. Rinse with cold water to stop the cooking process.
ARRANGE green beans in steamer basket over boiling water. Cover and steam 4 minutes or until crisp-tender. Plunge into ice water to stop the cooking process; drain. Repeat procedure with cauliflower and then broccoli.
PLACE vegetables on a lettuce-lined platter; cover and chill. Serve with Creamy Honey-Herb Dip.

Creamy Honey-Herb Dip:
MAKES 1¼ CUPS
PREP: 5 MIN.

If you don't have time to steam vegetables, serve this dip with a deli vegetable tray from the supermarket.

2 green onions
1 garlic clove
1 (8-ounce) container sour cream
1½ tablespoons stone-ground mustard
1 tablespoon honey
1 tablespoon cider vinegar
1 teaspoon dried tarragon
1 teaspoon anchovy paste (optional)

PROCESS first 7 ingredients and, if desired, anchovy paste in a food processor or blender until smooth; cover and chill.

Smoked Salmon Canapés

MAKES 2 DOZEN
PREP: 15 MIN., BAKE: 5 MIN.

1 French baguette
8 ounces thinly sliced smoked salmon
1 (8-ounce) package cream cheese, softened
½ cup sour cream
24 fresh dill sprigs

CUT baguette into 24 (½-inch-thick) slices, and place on a baking sheet.
BAKE at 400° for 5 minutes or until lightly toasted; remove to wire racks to cool.
CUT salmon into 24 pieces. Spread

Elegant Smoked Salmon Canapés call for just **5** ingredients and are ready in **20** minutes start to finish.

baguette slices evenly with cream cheese; top with salmon and sour cream. Place a dill sprig on each canapé.

Sesame-Maple Chicken Wings

MAKES 8 TO 10 APPETIZER SERVINGS
PREP: 20 MIN., CHILL: 2 HRS., COOK: 6 MIN.,
BAKE: 54 MIN.

⅓ cup maple syrup

¼ cup soy sauce

3 tablespoons sesame oil

1 tablespoon chopped fresh ginger

1 tablespoon chili oil

3 garlic cloves

4 pounds chicken wing pieces

2 tablespoons sesame seeds

PROCESS first 6 ingredients in a blender or food processor until smooth, stopping to scrape down sides. Place chicken in a shallow dish or large zip-top freezer bag; pour marinade over chicken. Cover or seal, and chill 2 hours.

REMOVE chicken from marinade, reserving marinade. Arrange chicken in a single layer on a lightly greased 15- x 10-inch jellyroll pan.

BRING reserved marinade to a boil in a small saucepan; boil 1 minute, and remove from heat.

BAKE chicken at 375° for 25 minutes; turn chicken, and bake 15 more minutes. Baste chicken with marinade; bake 7 minutes. Turn chicken, and baste with remaining marinade; sprinkle with sesame seeds, and bake 7 more minutes or until sesame seeds are golden.

Marinated Shrimp-and-Artichokes

MAKES 12 APPETIZER SERVINGS
PREP: 15 MIN., COOK: 5 MIN., CHILL: 8 HRS.

4½ pounds unpeeled, medium-size fresh shrimp

3 quarts water

1 (14-ounce) can quartered artichoke hearts, drained

⅓ cup olive oil

4 green onions, finely chopped

2 celery ribs, finely chopped

¼ cup finely chopped fresh parsley

1 teaspoon paprika

⅛ teaspoon salt

⅛ teaspoon pepper

1 teaspoon prepared horseradish

2½ tablespoons white vinegar

2½ tablespoons lemon juice

2 tablespoons Creole mustard

Dash of garlic salt

Lettuce leaves

BOIL shrimp in 3 quarts water 3 to 5 minutes or just until shrimp turn pink. Drain and rinse with cold water.

PEEL shrimp, and devein, if desired. Combine shrimp and artichoke hearts in a large bowl.

WHISK together oil and next 11 ingredients, and pour over shrimp mixture. Cover and chill 8 hours, stirring occasionally. Serve shrimp mixture over lettuce.

NOTE: You can cook the shrimp, in batches, with less water, or buy 2½ pounds peeled, steamed shrimp at the seafood counter at your supermarket, if desired.

Chewy Scotch Bars

MAKES 2½ DOZEN
PREP: 10 MIN., BAKE: 30 MIN.

2 cups semisweet chocolate morsels

2 tablespoons butter or margarine

1 (14-ounce) can sweetened condensed milk

1 cup butter or margarine, melted

1 (16-ounce) package light brown sugar

2 large eggs, lightly beaten

2 cups all-purpose flour

½ teaspoon salt

1 teaspoon vanilla extract

1 cup chopped pecans

MICROWAVE first 3 ingredients in a 2-quart microwave-safe bowl at HIGH 1½ minutes or until butter and chocolate melt, stirring twice.

STIR together 1 cup melted butter and brown sugar. Add eggs, stirring until blended. Stir in chocolate mixture, flour, and remaining ingredients. Pour into a greased 15- x 10-inch jellyroll pan.

BAKE at 350° for 30 minutes or until a wooden pick inserted in center comes out clean (do not overbake). Cool in pan on a wire rack, and cut into bars.

Soup Soothes the Soul

Chase away the chill—and a complicated to-do list—with these hearty soups.

Winter is the perfect time of year to invite friends over. To make guests feel welcome, offer an array of comforting soups. For a twist on the traditional party, set up a buffet of slow cookers or soup pots and let guests choose. These tempting recipes all start with Mirepoix to produce an extraordinary depth of flavor. Add baskets of bread and crackers, then provide a cheese plate and an ice-cream bar for dessert. What could be easier?

Mirepoix

MAKES ABOUT 3 CUPS
PREP: 10 MIN., COOK: 15 MIN.

3 tablespoons butter
1 cup diced celery
1 cup diced carrot
1 cup diced onion

MELT butter in a large skillet; add vegetables, and sauté 10 to 15 minutes or until tender. Cool.
STORE mixture in an airtight container in refrigerator up to 3 days, or freeze up to 2 months.

Mirepoix (mihr-PWAH)

This magical medley of aromatic vegetables was originally used to enhance the flavor of braised meats and sauces. Consisting of equal parts celery, onion, and carrot, mirepoix was first created in France during the 18th century. Over the years, this classic French foundation has become a popular addition to many ethnic soups. Some folks add garlic and bell pepper to the flavorful basic blend.

Old-Fashioned Vegetable-Beef Soup

MAKES 3 QUARTS
PREP: 35 MIN.; COOK: 2 HRS., 20 MIN.

⅔ cup all-purpose flour
1 teaspoon salt
1 teaspoon freshly ground pepper
2 pounds beef stew meat
2 garlic cloves, minced
3 tablespoons vegetable oil
2 (14-ounce) cans beef broth
1 cup Mirepoix (see recipe at left)
2 cups peeled, chopped potato
1 (28-ounce) can crushed tomatoes
1 (16-ounce) package frozen mixed vegetables, thawed
1 (16-ounce) package frozen white shoepeg corn, thawed
1 (15-ounce) can tomato sauce with garlic and herbs
1 tablespoon Worcestershire sauce

COMBINE flour, salt, and pepper in a large zip-top freezer bag; add beef. Seal and shake to coat.
SAUTÉ garlic in hot oil 1 minute; add beef, and cook 8 minutes, stirring occasionally, until browned.
ADD beef broth, Mirepoix, and remaining ingredients; bring to a boil. Reduce heat, and simmer 1½ to 2 hours or until beef is tender.

Set a company table with one of these delicious choices: (top, clockwise) Chicken-and-Wild Rice Soup With Fresh Mushrooms, Old-Fashioned Vegetable-Beef Soup, and Black Bean Soup topped with salsa.

Black Bean Soup

MAKES ABOUT 3 QUARTS
PREP: 25 MIN.; STAND: 1 HR.; COOK: 3 HRS., 20 MIN.

1 (1-pound) package dried black beans with seasoning packet
1 medium onion, chopped
1 large green bell pepper, chopped
4 garlic cloves, minced
3 tablespoons vegetable oil
4 (14-ounce) cans beef broth
1 smoked ham hock
1 cup Mirepoix (recipe, page 88)
1 tablespoon ground oregano
2 teaspoons salt
2 teaspoons freshly ground pepper
1 teaspoon ground cumin
1 teaspoon chili powder
2 bay leaves
1 pound hot smoked sausage, sliced
Salsa (optional)

REMOVE seasoning packet from beans, and set aside. Place beans in a Dutch oven; add water 2 inches above beans. Bring to a boil. Boil 1 minute; cover, remove from heat, and let stand 1 hour. Drain.

SAUTÉ onion, bell pepper, and garlic in hot oil in Dutch oven 4 to 5 minutes or until tender. Add beans, beef broth, and next 8 ingredients; bring to a boil. Reduce heat, and simmer, stirring occasionally, 1½ to 2 hours or until slightly thickened.

COOK smoked sausage and contents of seasoning packet in a skillet over medium-high heat until sausage is browned. Add to soup; cook, stirring often, 1 hour or until beans are tender. Remove and discard bay leaves. Serve soup with salsa, if desired.

Toast and Cornbread Stars

Cut white sandwich bread slices and 1-inch-thick cornbread with star-shaped cutters. (Trim cornbread, if necessary.) Brush with melted butter. Sprinkle lightly with grated Parmesan cheese and minced fresh parsley, if desired; place on a baking sheet. Bake at 375° for 10 to 15 minutes or until toasted.

Brunswick Stew

Brunswick Stew

MAKES 3½ QUARTS
PREP: 45 MIN., COOK: 2 HRS.

4 celery ribs
2 carrots
1 medium onion
2½ pounds chicken thighs, skinned
2 quarts water
2 teaspoons salt
1 teaspoon freshly ground pepper
5 whole cloves
1 pound shredded barbecued pork
2 cups peeled, chopped russet potato
¾ cup barbecue sauce
½ cup ketchup
¼ cup Worcestershire sauce
1 (10-ounce) package frozen lima beans, thawed
1 (16-ounce) package frozen white shoepeg corn, thawed
1 cup Mirepoix (recipe, page 88)
1 bay leaf

CUT celery, carrots, and onion in half; combine vegetables, chicken, and next 4 ingredients in a large stockpot. Bring mixture to a boil; reduce heat, and simmer 1 hour or until chicken is tender. Bone and shred chicken.

POUR broth through a wire-mesh strainer into a bowl, discarding vegetables; return broth to stockpot. Add chicken, pork, and remaining ingredients; bring to a boil. Reduce heat, and simmer, stirring occasionally, 1 hour or to desired thickness. Remove and discard bay leaf.

Chicken-and-Wild Rice Soup With Fresh Mushrooms

MAKES ABOUT 2½ QUARTS
PREP: 30 MIN., COOK: 1 HR.

1 (6-ounce) package long-grain and wild rice mix

⅔ cup all-purpose flour

1 teaspoon salt

1 teaspoon freshly ground pepper

6 skinned and boned chicken breasts, chopped

¼ cup butter or vegetable oil

2 garlic cloves, minced

¾ cup dry white wine

1 (8-ounce) package sliced fresh mushrooms

2 (14-ounce) cans chicken broth

1 cup Mirepoix (recipe, page 88)

2 cups half-and-half

PREPARE long-grain and wild rice mix according to package directions, and set aside.

COMBINE flour, salt, and pepper in a large zip-top plastic freezer bag. Add chicken; seal and toss to coat.

MELT butter in a large Dutch oven over medium-high heat; add garlic, and sauté 1 minute. Add chicken, and sauté until browned. Add wine and sliced mushrooms; cook, stirring often, 4 to 5 minutes.

STIR in broth and Mirepoix; reduce heat, and simmer, stirring occasionally, 10 to 15 minutes. Stir in rice and half-and-half; simmer, stirring occasionally, 20 to 30 minutes.

Chicken-and-Wild Rice Soup With Fresh Mushrooms and Toast Stars

A Feast Seasoned
With Goodwill

*Food and fun mark the end of Kwanzaa and the beginning
of a new year of togetherness.*

The Seven Principles of Kwanzaa

Seven candles—one black, three red, and three green—represent the seven principles of Kwanzaa. Each day, participants light one candle as they share ideas and memories and give thanks for friends and family.

1. Umoja (oo-MOE-jah) (unity): to strive for and maintain unity in the family, community, nation, and race.

2. Kujichagulia (koo-jee-cha-goo-LEE-a) (self-determination): to define ourselves, name ourselves, and create for ourselves rather than be defined, named, created for, and spoken for by others.

3. Ujima (oo-JEE-mae) (collective work and responsibility): to build and maintain our community together and to solve our sisters' and brothers' problems together.

4. Ujamaa (oo-JAH-mah) (cooperative economics): to build and maintain our own stores, shops, and other places of business and to profit from them as a community.

5. Nia (nee-AH) (purpose): to make our collective vocation the building and development of our community to restore our people to their traditional greatness.

6. Kuumba (koo-OOM-bah) (creativity): to do always as much as we can, in the way we can, in order to leave our community more beautiful and beneficial than when we inherited it.

7. Imani (ee-MAH-nee) (faith): to believe with all our heart in our people, our parents, our teachers, our leaders, and in the righteousness and victory of their struggle.

Kwanzaa takes a joyous look at the past and the promises for the future. From December 26 through January 1, African-Americans honor and give thanks for their ancestors' love, guidance, and wisdom. Although Kwanzaa is a nonreligious holiday, the warm atmosphere among participants is very spiritual. Each evening a new candle is lit, and one of the seven principles is defined and explored.

The holiday comes to a festive conclusion with a feast. A buffet of gifts from the Earth—grains, vegetables, and fruits—is spread for all to enjoy. Begin with samples from our table, and add your family's favorites. Fancy African attire and decorations are not essential. All you need is love in your heart and the desire to share it.

Chicken With Onions

MAKES 8 SERVINGS
PREP: 15 MIN., COOK: 24 MIN.

3 cups uncooked long-grain rice
8 skinned and boned chicken breasts
2 teaspoons salt
2 to 3 teaspoons dried crushed red pepper
2 tablespoons bacon drippings
4 large onions, thinly sliced (6 cups)

COOK rice according to package directions. Set aside, and keep warm.
SPRINKLE chicken breasts with salt and crushed red pepper.
BROWN chicken breasts, 4 at a time, in hot bacon drippings in a large skillet over high heat 2 minutes. Remove chicken from skillet.
ADD onion slices to skillet, and sauté 10 minutes. Return chicken breasts to skillet, and cook 10 more minutes. Serve with hot cooked rice.

(left) Southern dishes, such as Collard Greens Salad, are the choice of many celebrants because they emphasize remembrance.

Spicy Squash Soup isn't too fiery, so if you prefer a little more heat, simply add a bit more crushed red pepper.

Spicy Squash Soup

MAKES 7 CUPS
PREP: 30 MIN., COOK: 45 MIN.

3 (14-ounce) cans chicken broth
1 large onion, chopped
½ to 1 teaspoon dried crushed red pepper
3 cups peeled, cubed acorn squash (about 1¼ pounds)*
½ teaspoon salt
3 cups water
½ cup uncooked long-grain rice
¼ cup creamy peanut butter
Garnish: chopped fresh parsley

BRING ¼ cup chicken broth, onion, and crushed red pepper to a boil in a large saucepan; cook 5 minutes or until onion is tender. Add remaining broth, squash, salt, and 3 cups water; bring to a boil. Cover, reduce heat, and simmer 20 minutes. Add rice; cover and simmer 20 more minutes or until squash and rice are tender.
PROCESS peanut butter and half of soup in a blender or food processor until smooth, stopping to scrape down sides; pour into a large bowl. Process remaining soup until smooth; add to bowl, stirring well. Ladle into individual bowls. Garnish, if desired.
*Substitute butternut squash, if desired.

Collard Greens Salad

MAKES 8 TO 10 SERVINGS
PREP: 35 MIN., CHILL: 1 HR.

12 pounds fresh collard greens, washed, trimmed, and shredded
3 small carrots, shredded
1 onion, minced
3 garlic cloves, minced
¼ cup olive oil
3 tablespoons apple cider vinegar
½ teaspoon dried oregano

TOSS together all ingredients in a large bowl. Chill 1 hour.

Creamed-Corn Cornbread

MAKES 9 SERVINGS
PREP: 15 MIN., BAKE: 22 MIN.

1 cup yellow cornmeal
¾ cup all-purpose flour
1 tablespoon sugar
1 tablespoon baking powder
½ teaspoon salt
¾ cup milk
1 large egg
2 tablespoons vegetable oil
1 (8½-ounce) can cream-style corn
2 to 3 teaspoons vegetable oil or bacon drippings

COMBINE first 5 ingredients in a bowl; make a well in center of mixture. Stir together milk and next 3 ingredients; add to dry ingredients, stirring just until dry ingredients are moistened.
COAT bottom and sides of a 9-inch cast-iron skillet with vegetable oil or bacon drippings. Place skillet in a 450° oven for 5 minutes. Remove from oven, and immediately spoon cornbread batter into skillet.
BAKE at 450° for 20 to 22 minutes or until a wooden pick inserted in center comes out clean.
NOTE: To reduce fat and calories, substitute ¾ cup fat-free milk for whole milk and ¼ cup egg substitute for 1 large egg.

Dressed Up Supper Club

Make the last supper club gathering of the year one to be remembered.

Holidays are the time many supper club groups pull out all the stops and gather for a fancy dinner party. Here's a plan to help you make it fun and fabulous from the first thought of "let's plan a special party," to the last "wow, that was an evening to remember."

A Magnificent Meal
Serves 6

Hot Spiced Wine

Peanutty Party Mix

Warmed Cranberry Brie

Pear, Jícama, and Snow Pea Salad With Basil-Balsamic Vinaigrette

Cajun Beef Fillets With Parmesan Grits

Asparagus With Lemon

Chocolate-Covered Cherry Pie

Hot Spiced Wine

MAKES 9 CUPS
PREP: 5 MIN., COOK: 20 MIN.

To serve, use a tempered glass, heatproof pitcher, a thermal carafe, or simply return mixture to Dutch oven and ladle into mugs.

2 (750-milliliter) bottles red wine
2 cups apple juice
1 cup sugar
6 tablespoons mulling spices

BRING all ingredients to a boil in a Dutch oven; reduce heat, and simmer 15 minutes. Pour mixture through a wire-mesh strainer into a pitcher, discarding mulling spices. Serve wine hot.
NOTE: For best results, use a fruity red wine, such as a Beaujolais or Pinot Noir.

Here's a conversation-friendly table setting. One tall element catches guests' attention as they enter the room, while the others are low enough to see and talk over.

Peanutty Party Mix

MAKES ABOUT 12 CUPS
PREP: 10 MIN., BAKE: 25 MIN.

1 (12-ounce) package chow mein noodles
2 cups dry-roasted or honey-roasted peanuts
2 cups uncooked regular oats
½ cup butter or margarine
1 tablespoon sesame oil
¼ cup firmly packed brown sugar
1 (¾-ounce) envelope hot-and-spicy fried rice seasoning mix
1 (6-ounce) package sweetened dried cranberries

COMBINE first 3 ingredients in a large bowl; set aside.
MELT butter with oil in a small saucepan over medium heat; stir in sugar and seasoning mix, and cook, stirring constantly, 5 minutes or until sugar dissolves. Pour sugar mixture evenly over peanut mixture in bowl; toss to coat. Spread mixture in an even layer in a lightly greased 15- x 10-inch jellyroll pan.
BAKE at 300° for 25 minutes, stirring twice. Remove from oven, and stir in cranberries. Cool completely in pan on a wire rack. Store in an airtight container.
NOTE: For testing purposes only, we used Sun-Bird Hot & Spicy Fried Rice Authentic Oriental Seasoning Mix.

Serve small bowls of Peanutty Party Mix for predinner nibbles. Then give guests a bag of this spicy treat to take home.

COOK snow pea pods in boiling salted water to cover 30 seconds or until crisp-tender; drain. Plunge into ice water to stop the cooking process; drain.

CUT peas, pear, and jícama into thin strips; gently toss pear with lemon juice.

LAYER spinach, snow peas, pear, and jícama; sprinkle with almonds. Serve with Basil-Balsamic Vinaigrette.

Basil-Balsamic Vinaigrette:
MAKES 1 CUP
PREP: 10 MIN.

¼ cup balsamic vinegar
1 teaspoon Dijon mustard
1 garlic clove
1 teaspoon sugar
¼ teaspoon coarsely ground pepper
¾ cup olive oil
2 green onions, chopped
2 tablespoons chopped fresh basil

PROCESS first 5 ingredients in a blender or food processor until smooth, stopping to scrape down sides. Gradually add olive oil in a slow, steady stream, and process mixture until well blended. Stir in green onions and basil.

Paper-thin slices of pear and jícama top this spinach-based Pear, Jícama, and Snow Pea Salad With Basil-Balsamic Vinaigrette.

To simplify the appetizer course, prepare several makings of just one recipe, such as Warmed Cranberry Brie. Remember, an appetizer is a "tease," and there's more great food to enjoy.

Warmed Cranberry Brie

MAKES 6 APPETIZER SERVINGS
PREP: 10 MIN., BAKE: 5 MIN.

Try tossing pear and apple slices in pineapple juice to keep them from turning brown. It works as well as lemon juice and has a sweeter flavor.

1 (16-ounce) round Brie
1 (16-ounce) can whole-berry cranberry sauce
¼ cup firmly packed brown sugar
2 tablespoons spiced rum*
½ teaspoon ground nutmeg
¼ cup chopped pecans, toasted
French bread baguette slices, toasted
Apple and pear slices
Red grape clusters

TRIM rind from top of Brie, leaving a ⅓-inch border on top.

PLACE Brie on a baking sheet.

STIR together cranberry sauce and next 3 ingredients; spread mixture evenly over Brie. Sprinkle evenly with pecans.

BAKE at 500° for 5 minutes. Serve with toasted baguette slices, apple and pear slices, and red grapes.

*Substitute 2 tablespoons orange juice for spiced rum.

Pear, Jícama, and Snow Pea Salad With Basil-Balsamic Vinaigrette

MAKES 6 TO 8 SERVINGS
PREP: 25 MIN., COOK: 30 SECONDS

Jícama, often nicknamed Mexican potato, is a tropical root vegetable with a sweet, nutty flavor.

1 cup fresh snow pea pods
1 pear, peeled
1 small jícama, peeled
¾ teaspoon lemon juice
1 (6-ounce) package baby spinach, sliced
1 (2-ounce) package sliced almonds, toasted
Basil-Balsamic Vinaigrette

Cajun Beef Fillets With Parmesan Grits look fancy, but they're surprisingly easy to make.

Cajun Beef Fillets With Parmesan Grits

MAKES 6 SERVINGS
PREP: 15 MIN., COOK: 13 MIN., BAKE: 10 MIN.

We suggest a Cabernet Sauvignon or Shiraz for preparing and serving with the beef fillets.

6 (7- to 8-ounce) beef tenderloin fillets
3 tablespoons Cajun seasoning, divided
2½ tablespoons olive oil, divided
4 large shallots, chopped
1 pound assorted fresh mushrooms, sliced
¾ cup dry red wine
1 (14-ounce) can beef broth
2 tablespoons cornstarch
Parmesan Grits

RUB fillets evenly on all sides with 2 tablespoons Cajun seasoning.
BROWN fillets in 1½ tablespoons hot oil in a large skillet over medium-high heat 2 to 3 minutes on each side.

Remove fillets to a baking dish, reserving drippings in skillet.
BAKE fillets at 350° for 8 to 10 minutes or to desired degree of doneness. Keep warm.
ADD shallots and remaining 1 tablespoon oil to drippings in skillet. Sauté over medium-high heat 1 minute. Add mushrooms and remaining 1 tablespoon Cajun seasoning, and sauté 3 minutes or until tender. Add red wine, and cook, stirring often, 2 minutes or until liquid is reduced by half.
STIR together beef broth and cornstarch; stir into mushroom mixture in skillet; bring to a boil, and cook, stirring often, 1 minute.
SERVE fillets over Parmesan Grits; spoon mushroom sauce over fillets.
NOTE: For testing purposes only, we used McCormick Gourmet Collection Cajun Seasoning.

Parmesan Grits:

MAKES 6 SERVINGS
PREP: 5 MIN., COOK: 20 MIN.

If the grits thicken too much, add milk, a little at a time, to desired consistency.

2 cups water
2 cups milk
½ teaspoon salt
1 cup uncooked regular grits
1 cup shredded Parmesan cheese
3 tablespoons prepared horseradish
¼ teaspoon ground red pepper

BRING first 3 ingredients to a boil in a heavy 3-quart saucepan over medium-high heat; gradually stir in grits. Return to a boil; cover, reduce heat, and simmer, stirring often, 20 minutes. Stir in cheese, horseradish, and ground red pepper, stirring until cheese melts. Serve immediately.

Asparagus With Lemon

MAKES 6 TO 8 SERVINGS
PREP: 15 MIN., COOK: 10 MIN.

Asparagus can be cooked the day before the party and refrigerated. For an extra touch, garnish with shaved Parmesan cheese.

2 pounds fresh asparagus
2 tablespoons butter or margarine
¼ cup lemon juice
½ teaspoon salt

SNAP off tough ends of asparagus; remove scales from stalks with a vegetable peeler, if desired.

COOK asparagus in boiling water to cover 5 minutes or until crisp-tender; drain. Plunge into ice water to stop the cooking process; drain.

MELT butter in a skillet over medium heat; stir in lemon juice and salt. Add asparagus; cook just until heated. Serve immediately.

For simple place cards, cut slits in the tops of small green apples, and tuck berries, small pieces of curly willow, and name cards into slits. (Make sure guests know that the apple place card holders are for display only and are not edible.)

Chocolate-covered cherry candy, a classic confection for holiday gift giving, inspired this yummy, make-ahead Chocolate-Covered Cherry Pie.

Chocolate-Covered Cherry Pie

MAKES 8 SERVINGS
PREP: 35 MIN.; BAKE: 30 MIN.;
CHILL: 8 HRS., 15 MIN.; STAND: 10 MIN.

Make this dessert the day before. Keep chocolate-covered cherries in an airtight container.

2 cups semisweet chocolate morsels
½ cup whipping cream
¼ cup butter or margarine, cut into pieces
1 (6-ounce) ready-made chocolate crumb piecrust
1 (21-ounce) can cherry pie filling
1 (8-ounce) package cream cheese, softened
⅓ cup powdered sugar
1 large egg
¼ teaspoon almond extract
16 maraschino cherries with stems
2 cups thawed whipped topping or sweetened whipped cream

MICROWAVE chocolate morsels and cream in a glass bowl at MEDIUM (50% power) 1 to 2 minutes or until chocolate begins to melt. Whisk in butter until smooth. Let cool, whisking occasionally, 5 to 10 minutes or to desired spreading consistency.

SPOON half of chocolate mixture into piecrust. Cover and chill remaining chocolate mixture.

SPOON cherry pie filling evenly over chocolate mixture in piecrust. Place piecrust on a baking sheet, and set aside.

BEAT cream cheese and next 3 ingredients at medium speed with an electric mixer until smooth. Pour cream cheese mixture evenly over cherry pie filling mixture. (Piecrust will be full, but contents will not overflow when baking.)

BAKE at 350° for 30 minutes or until center is set. Remove from oven, and cool on a wire rack. Cover and chill 8 hours.

DRAIN stemmed cherries on paper towels; pat dry.

MICROWAVE reserved chocolate mixture at MEDIUM (50% power) 1 minute. Remove from microwave, and stir until spreading consistency, reheating as necessary.

DIP stemmed cherries in chocolate mixture, and place on a baking sheet lined with wax paper; chill for 15 minutes.

SPREAD remaining chocolate mixture evenly over pie. Spoon 8 dollops of whipped topping or cream around outer edge of pie; place 2 chocolate covered-cherries in center of each dollop. Serve immediately.

Create a Simple, Yet Stunning, Centerpiece

For a table of six guests, you'll need one tulip topiary with small containers of roses and hypericum berries beside it. For larger tables, you may need several topiaries placed down the center of the table.

■ To assemble this flower topiary, soak a block of florist foam (often called Oasis) in water for one to two hours or until it's heavy. Trim foam, using a knife, to fit container. Insert tulips, one stem at a time, into center of foam. Don't push flowers in as a cluster; the stems may break. Insert curly willow branch, and tie to tulip stems with ribbon for support.

Tip: Generally the height of the tallest flowers should be double the height of the container.

■ Insert roses into the foam. Turn container so that all sides are evenly filled with roses; tie stems together with ribbon.

Tip: You may need to pull the ribbon tight (like you were tying your shoes) to get the cluster effect.

■ Fill in the base with bright green Kermit mums and hypericum berries. Cover any exposed foam with sheet moss.

Tip: The little bit of moss you need may be growing in a shady portion of your yard. Use a kitchen utensil, like a metal pancake turner, to peel moss from the ground.

Charmed Wine Glasses

To help guests keep track of their wine glass, tie strands of beads, in one color for each guest, around wine goblet stems. Beads, tiny jingle bells, and thin ribbon or cording are available at local craft stores.

Buffet Menu
Serves 8
White Sangría Fizz
Toasted Oat Scones
Strawberry-Almond Cream Cheese
Southwestern Egg Casserole
Roasted Red Potato Bites
Cherry Tomato Salad
Cornmeal-Pecan Pancakes
Champagne Punch

Host a Christmas Brunch

Deck your table for a festive midday meal with family and friends

Entertain differently this year, and host a midday open house brunch for neighbors, friends, and family. Let your budget and energy determine whether it'll be elaborately formal or comfortably laid-back. Use simple flowers from the supermarket to create welcoming wreaths and knockout centerpieces that will suit any party. Take time to enjoy your own party with this menu for a bountiful buffet. It's full of shortcuts and make-ahead recipes that help keep holidays fun.

White Sangría Fizz

MAKES 8 SERVINGS
PREP: 5 MIN., CHILL: 8 HRS.

Stir up this before bedtime, and add sparkling water just before serving.

1 cup fresh orange juice
½ cup sugar
1 (750-milliliter) bottle dry white wine
1½ cups sparkling water, chilled
Garnishes: lime, orange, and lemon wedges

STIR together orange juice and sugar in a large pitcher until sugar dissolves. Stir in wine; cover and chill 8 hours.

STIR sparkling water into wine mixture just before serving. Garnish, if desired.

Toasted Oat Scones with Strawberry-Almond Cream Cheese get the party off to a delicious start.

White Sangría Fizz

Toasted Oat Scones

MAKES 1 DOZEN
PREP: 20 MIN., BAKE: 14 MIN.

Serve with Strawberry-Almond Cream Cheese (recipe, page 102).

1¼ cups quick-cooking oats, uncooked
1½ cups all-purpose flour
½ cup sugar
2 teaspoons baking powder
½ teaspoon salt
½ teaspoon ground cinnamon
¼ teaspoon baking soda
¼ cup butter or margarine, cut up
½ cup sweetened dried cranberries
½ cup fat-free buttermilk
½ cup applesauce
1 teaspoon vanilla extract
2 teaspoons butter or margarine, melted
1 teaspoon sugar

PLACE oats on a lightly greased baking sheet.

BAKE at 450° for 3 minutes or until lightly toasted, stirring once. Cool completely.

COMBINE 1 cup toasted oats, 1½ cups flour, and next 5 ingredients; cut in ¼ cup butter with a pastry blender until crumbly. Add dried cranberries, and toss well. Add buttermilk, applesauce, and vanilla, stirring just until dry ingredients are moistened.

TURN dough out onto a lightly floured surface; knead lightly 4 times. Pat dough into a 9-inch circle on a lightly greased baking sheet. Brush with melted butter; sprinkle with remaining ¼ cup toasted oats and 1 teaspoon sugar.

BAKE at 450° for 11 minutes or until golden. Serve warm.

Strawberry-Almond Cream Cheese

MAKES APPROXIMATELY 1¼ CUPS
PREP: 10 MIN., CHILL: 1 HR.

*Serve this hearty cream cheese as a
sweet topping for scones, bagels,
or English muffins.*

1 (8-ounce) package cream cheese, softened
3 tablespoons powdered sugar
¾ teaspoon almond extract
½ cup chopped fresh strawberries (about 8
   large strawberries)

PROCESS first 3 ingredients in a food
processor just until blended. (Do not
overprocess or mixture will be thin.)
ADD strawberries; process just until
blended. Cover; chill at least 1 hour.

Southwestern Egg Casserole

MAKES 12 SERVINGS
PREP: 15 MIN.; CHILL: 8 HRS.; BAKE: 1 HR., 10 MIN.;
STAND: 5 MIN.

*Assemble this casserole the night before,
and put it in the oven 30 minutes
before your guests arrive. It will finish
baking while your guests sip on
White Sangría Fizz, page 101, and
Champagne Punch, facing page.*

12 (5-inch) corn tortillas, cut into 1-inch
   strips and divided
10 large eggs
1 cup half-and-half
1 (12-ounce) container 1% low-fat cottage
   cheese
¾ teaspoon salt
½ teaspoon pepper
1 cup (4 ounces) shredded Mexican cheese
   blend
4 green onions, thinly sliced
1½ cups salsa

PLACE tortilla strips on an ungreased
baking sheet.
BAKE at 325° for 10 minutes or until
crisp; cool.

Southwestern Egg Casserole topped with salsa and baked tortilla strips, Roasted Red Potato Bites, and Cherry Tomato Salad make an attractive holiday meal.

WHISK eggs in a large bowl; stir in
half-and-half and next 3 ingredients.
Stir in three-fourths of the tortilla
strips, 1 cup cheese, and green
onions. Pour mixture into a lightly
greased 13- x 9-inch baking dish.
Cover with foil, and chill 8 hours.
BAKE casserole, covered, at 325° for
40 minutes. Uncover and bake 20
more minutes or just until set.
Remove casserole from oven, and let
stand 5 minutes. (Casserole will continue to get firm as it cools.)
CUT casserole into 12 squares. Spoon
2 tablespoons salsa over each serving;
sprinkle with remaining tortilla strips.

Roasted Red Potato Bites

MAKES 2 DOZEN
PREP: 25 MIN., BAKE: 45 MIN.,
BROIL: 5 MIN.

12 small red potatoes (about 1½ to 2 pounds)
1 tablespoon olive oil
½ cup mayonnaise
1 cup (4 ounces) shredded Cheddar cheese
   blend
½ pound bacon, cooked and crumbled
½ cup minced green onions
2 tablespoons chopped fresh or 2 teaspoons
   dried basil

RUB potatoes with olive oil, and
place on an ungreased baking sheet.

BAKE at 400° for 45 minutes or until
tender. Let cool.
CUT each potato in half crosswise; cut
a thin slice from bottom of each half,
forming a base for potatoes to stand
on, if necessary. Scoop out pulp,
leaving at least a ¼-inch-thick shell;
reserve pulp.
STIR together reserved potato pulp, ½
cup mayonnaise, 1 cup shredded
Cheddar cheese blend, and next 3
ingredients in a large bowl. Spoon
mixture evenly into each potato shell.
Place on a lightly greased baking sheet.
BROIL potato bites 5 inches from heat
3 to 5 minutes or until lightly
browned. Serve warm.

Roasted Red Potato Bites filled with
bacon, cheese, and green onions
are like miniature twice-baked
potatoes.

Tie fresh cut flowers with ribbon for beautiful napkin rings.

Arrange flatware decoratively if space permits.

No-cook Cherry Tomato Salad is ready with just 15 minutes prep time. Make it ahead, and chill for maximum flavor.

Cherry Tomato Salad

MAKES 8 SERVINGS
PREP: 15 MIN., CHILL: 1 HR.

4 pints cherry tomatoes (about 3 pounds), halved
2 tablespoons white wine vinegar
2 tablespoons olive oil
1 teaspoon salt
½ teaspoon pepper
1 garlic clove, finely chopped
¼ cup chopped fresh mint

STIR together first 6 ingredients in a large bowl. Add mint, tossing gently to coat. Cover and chill 1 hour.

Cornmeal-Pecan Pancakes

MAKES 8 SERVINGS
PREP: 25 MIN., COOK: 20 MIN.

1 cup all-purpose flour
½ cup yellow cornmeal
¼ cup diced pecans, toasted
1 tablespoon sugar
1 tablespoon baking powder
½ teaspoon baking soda
½ teaspoon salt
2 cups low-fat buttermilk
1 tablespoon vegetable oil
1 large egg
¾ cup maple syrup

STIR together first 7 ingredients. WHISK together buttermilk, oil, and egg. Add to flour mixture, stirring just until moistened.

POUR about ¼ cup batter for each pancake onto a hot nonstick griddle or skillet.

COOK pancakes until tops are covered with bubbles and edges look cooked; turn and cook other side. Serve immediately with maple syrup.

Champagne Punch

MAKES 12 CUPS
PREP: 5 MIN.

This refreshing and beautiful punch is not just for Christmas; it's perfect for many occasions from bridal and baby showers to teas and reunions.

3 cups red fruit punch, chilled
3 cups unsweetened pineapple juice, chilled
3 cups white grape juice, chilled
1 (750-milliliter) bottle pink champagne, chilled*

STIR together all ingredients, and serve immediately.

NOTE: For testing purposes only, we used Hawaiian Punch Red Fruit Punch.

*Substitute 2 (12-ounce) cans ginger ale, chilled, for pink champagne.

Champagne Punch

Party at Your Fingertips

With a little organization, you'll be ready to party like a pro.

The secret to having a successful party is being prepared. Get ready by creating your own party pantry filled with essentials for hosting any style party at any time. It's easier than you think.

Take over a closet, a bookcase, or even freestanding shelves in your garage to gather all your party goods. Each one can easily be transformed to suit your storage needs. Converting a linen closet with shelves is the simplest choice. You can also add shelves to the closet in your spare bedroom. (Hire a handyman, or do it yourself. Closet organizers are readily available at home improvement stores.) If these aren't options, buy bookcases and hang inexpensive curtain panels on the front to keep the dust bunnies away. An open shelving unit will need fabric panels on at least 3 sides. Line the shelves in your chosen space with paper or protective liners.

When the shelves are ready, take stock of all your entertaining gear. Group similar items together. Here are a few examples to help with your sorting:

Table linens: tablecloths, napkins, and towels. Separate the fabric from the paper items.

Formal dining: good china, crystal, silver serving pieces, and flatware.

Casual dining: casual dishes, glasses, and serving pieces.

Now you're ready to fill the shelves. For the pieces you reach for all the time when entertaining, store in the middle for effortless access. Place seasonal or infrequently used items on the top or bottom shelves. You may want to take inventory of each shelf for a quick reference.

Shop for casual, inexpensive pieces to add each season to keep your look current.

Party Essentials

- **Various glassware:** Water, wine, champagne, martini, margarita, and pilsner. Glasses also can be used to serve desserts, iced tea, or punch. Select insulated plastic cups and fun acrylic glassware for safety outdoors.

Plate rack

- **China:** Purchase padded storage containers to protect fine china.
- **Charger plates**
- **Plate rack:** To store dishes with ease.
- **Flatware and serving utensils:** Choose wooden, metal, or brightly colored styles that are different from your everyday stainless.
- **Silver:** Serving trays, casserole caddies, bowls, and mint julep glasses. Buy chemically treated antitarnish bags and yards of antitarnish cloth to line the shelf and cover all pieces.

Flatware

- **Ice bucket**
- **Wine cooler or bucket**

- **Party tub:** Ice drinks of all kinds, or have guests place birthday presents inside when they arrive.
- **Footed cake pedestal**
- **Trifle bowl**
- **Linens:** Start with white or ivory, and add colors and fun prints that compliment your china and everyday dishes.
- **Napkins:** Buy cloth napkins to match tablecloths. Select a rainbow of solid-colored dinner-, luncheon-, and cocktail-sized napkins made of fabric or paper. Also, look for those with colorful or humorous prints.
- **Place mats:** Select a variety of coordinating fabrics, natural fibers, and laminate for easy cleanup.
- **Tea or kitchen towels:** Keep a few to use when entertaining. Also, use to line baskets for bread or chips.
- **Candles:** Find tapers, pillars, tea lights, and votives of all colors on sale to stock up. Choose regular and dripless varieties.
- **Candlesticks:** Brass, silver, wrought iron, and glass. Empty Chianti bottles

are great candleholders for Italian-themed entertaining. For added charm, let the wax collect down the neck and sides.

- **Votive holders:** Collect these by the dozen, and scatter on the dining table, in the foyer, outdoors on the deck, and in the guest powder room.
- **Baskets:** All shapes and sizes to hold everything from bread to flowers to ice.
- **Vases:** Begin with one tall, five short, and three pitchers, which can serve beverages or be filled with

Ribbon

flowers for a centerpiece.

- **Ribbon:** Stock up on spools of ribbon, raffia, wired ribbon, string, and lengths of rope. Most of these items can be bought inexpensively at after-season sales.
- **Small decorative, whimsical items:** Seashells, small figurines, paper umbrellas, confetti, birdcages, and terra-cotta pots.

Glasses Galore

A good starting point for entertaining is to buy 8 each of these glasses.

- **Wine:** A long-stemmed glass with a tulip shape. It's slightly smaller at the rim; generally holds about 8 ounces.
- **Iced tea:** Similar to a wine glass, but with a much shorter stem and larger bowl. Also used to serve water, soft drinks, or other drinks served over ice.
- **Double old-fashioned:** Straight-sided, heavy-bottomed glass used for beverages served during the cocktail hour rather than at a seated meal.
- **Balloon or bubble:** A long-stemmed glass with a very large round bowl used to serve red wines.

Taking Care of Glassware

- Put heavier, everyday pieces in the dishwasher, but wash fine crystal by hand in a sink lined with a towel or rubber mat to prevent breakage. Remove your rings and bracelets to avoid scratching glasses. Wash and rinse one piece at a time. Never place ice-cold glasses in hot dishwater because the temperature change can cause the glass to crack.
- Store stemmed glasses with the bowls up. Leave enough space between glasses to avoid scratches or chips from touching one another. For extra protection, line shelves with a soft cloth or nonskid liner.
- If glassware develops a cloudy look, rub it with lemon juice; then wash it in a water-vinegar solution, and rinse.

or pasta, place that on the buffet first. Place dressings, sauces, and other condiments beside the food they complement. Place napkins and eating utensils at the end so guests won't have to juggle them as they serve themselves.

When both hands are needed to serve a dish, leave space in front of the serving container for guests to set down their plates.

If the buffet space accommodates only the food, place plates, silverware, and napkins on a separate table nearby. Arrange flatware in single rows, on top of individual napkins, or wrapped in a bundle inside each napkin.

Serve beverages from a side table so guests can seat themselves and return for drinks.

Ready, Set, Buffet

10 Secrets to Easy Entertaining

Buffet entertaining, where guests serve themselves, is a popular choice for any occasion. This entertaining style allows you to mingle with guests and replenish serving containers as needed. It also allows you to serve a larger number of guests. Choose menus and themes appropriate to the occasion and your budget, space, and style.

1 Choose the Best Spot

A buffet can be set up on a dining table or other large surface, such as a chest, kitchen counter, sideboard, library table, or a picnic table outside. Place the table where it's most convenient for serving, clearing, and traffic flow. A minimum space of 18 inches is required for guests to walk between pieces of furniture. Allow for easy circulation before, during, and after the meal so guests who have served themselves don't cross paths with those waiting in line.

2 Organize the Flow

Arrange plates, food, and serving utensils on the buffet in logical order so guests can serve themselves without backtracking. Plates belong at the beginning, followed by the entrée, vegetables, salad, and bread. If you're serving the entrée over rice

3 Plan a Workable Menu

Make sure the food on the menu is simple to serve and eat. If guests will be seated at tables while eating, food that requires a knife and fork is appropriate. Guests who'll be seated in chairs with plates on their laps appreciate food they can eat with a fork. When seating space is limited and guests will have to stand, a menu consisting of finger foods is the best option.

One main dish is sufficient. If more than one is offered, have plenty of each on hand. Guests tend to take a little of each.

When the guest list is large and some of the food is served hot, make two or three casseroles of each rather than one very large dish; that way food stays hot for those guests at the end of the line.

4 Dress It Up With Pretty, Practical Fabrics

Fine table coverings, heirloom pieces, damask, linen, and sheer organdy toppers are typically used for formal occasions. For casual or less formal events, look around your home for ideas. Try using a quilt, fabrics that complement the dishes, burlap, crisp cotton sheets, or a bed of rye grass to create the desired look. Always protect surfaces from hot and cold temperatures, moisture, and spills by first placing a protective barrier, such as a table pad or sheets of plastic.

5 Stack It Up

Add interest on the buffet by elevating several dishes to create levels. A cake pedestal or a shallow-footed bowl are perfect choices to hold food or other serving pieces. Less attractive items used for height may be hidden under drapes of fabric for the same effect. Have a trial run to set the buffet and work free of deadlines and distractions. You won't know if an arrangement will work until you try it.

When you find your desired look, draw the shape of the buffet surface (rectangle, square, circle) with all items needed listed as a reference. Set the table the day before your event. Place serving pieces and utensils on the table, and put the name of the recipe on a sticky note in each serving dish.

6 Add Beauty With Centerpieces

Centerpieces should contribute to the mood of the occasion rather than dominating the table; otherwise, with the many serving pieces, the table will be too crowded. Also, if a centerpiece is used on a table, be sure it isn't too large or tall to obstruct the view of each guest.

If the buffet is placed against a wall, create an asymmetrical effect by placing the centerpiece at the end of the buffet line. One arrangement in the center is best for circular tables. Scatter several arrangements down the middle of a rectangular table. Consider fresh flowers, fruits, nuts, greenery, potted bedding plants, ferns, and figurines for use in centerpieces.

7 Go for Mood

The type of lighting you choose can help establish the mood and atmosphere. A rheostat or dimmer switch that lowers overhead lighting is a necessity in a dining room. Remember to use candles only after dusk, and do not put candles on the table unless they'll be lit. Make sure all candles are lit before guests arrive. Tapered candles are usually used for a dressier table, while votive candles will work for any style table. Choose votive holders to help carry out a theme.

8 Set a Sideboard

When the group you're entertaining is small and will be seated, a sideboard is an excellent serving solution. Set the table with napkins, flatware, breads, beverages, and any condiments. Consider using this arrangement when guests have access to food from only one side. This grouping also works using a large baker's rack, a kitchen counter, or a narrow table against a wall.

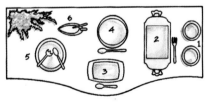

Sideboard

1. dinner plates
2. entrée
3. vegetable
4. vegetable
5. salad
6. sauce or salad dressing

9 Set a Buffet for a Large Group

Good traffic flow is the key to serving a large group. A dining table or a freestanding buffet table with identical serving lines on each side will handle a crowd.

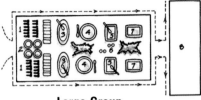

Large Group

1. dinner forks and napkins
2. dinner plates
3. entrée
4. vegetable
5. salad
6. salt and pepper shakers
7. bread
8. beverages

10 Set a Round Buffet

A single round table works for smaller groups. To accommodate more guests and, if space allows, group several tables together or scatter throughout for easy access.

Round

1. dinner forks and napkins
2. dinner plates
3. entrée
4. vegetable
5. salad
6. salt and pepper shakers
7. bread

From Ordinary
to Extraordinary

Savvy food and decorating ideas dress up a gathering.

Easy embellishments ensure you get the accolades you deserve. Enticing garnishes, unique serving ideas, and eye-pleasing arrangements are some of the simple techniques that can make your party exceptional.

Add Simple Garnishes

There are many ways to dress up a dish with garnishes that add color and texture to the plate. You can decorate with fresh herbs, vegetables, or fruits that are used in that recipe. A dollop of sour cream or sprinkle of bacon also can add visual interest, as well as flavor.

Garnish idea;
for recipe see
page 57

Present with Pizzazz

If the occasion calls for a formal approach, use stemware to add an air of refinement to an otherwise simple recipe. For example, you could serve mashed potatoes in martini glasses with a choice of toppings, or present banana pudding in crystal goblets. If the setting is more casual, let the party's theme inspire prizewinning presentations. Here are few simple recipes and ideas for unique presentations.

Apricot-
Chicken Salad

Apricot-Chicken Salad

MAKES 6 SERVINGS
PREP: 25 MIN.

Apricot-Chicken Salad becomes an elegant entrée when served in stemmed dessert bowls and stacked on a glass cake stand. Fresh apricot slices and herb sprigs make up the garnish.

½ cup plain yogurt	3 cups chopped cooked chicken
¼ cup mayonnaise	1 cup sliced almonds, toasted
3 tablespoons apricot preserves	¾ cup sliced celery
2 teaspoons grated fresh ginger	1 (6-ounce) package dried
½ teaspoon salt	apricots, chopped
½ teaspoon freshly ground	Garnishes: fresh apricot slices,
pepper	fresh thyme sprigs

WHISK together first 6 ingredients in a large bowl; add chicken and next 3 ingredients, tossing gently. Chill until ready to serve. Garnish, if desired.

Beehive Butter

Beehive Butter

MAKES 3 CUPS
PREP: 20 MIN., CHILL: 2 HRS.

Beehive Butter attracts brunch guests to a plate of ham biscuits. This scrumptious spread is easily molded into a hivelike mound that's perfect for a spring gathering. Or scoop this spread from a crock, if you prefer.

1½ cups butter, softened
½ cup spicy brown mustard
1 cup finely chopped pecans, toasted

1 pecan half
Garnishes: fresh herbs, edible flower petals

STIR together first 3 ingredients. Shape butter mixture into a beehive shape. Smooth mound with a spatula or rounded knife. Use fork tines to form grooves around mound. Insert pecan half near the base to make a "door." Cover and chill at least 2 hours. Garnish, if desired.

Barbecue Sundae

Barbecue Sundae

MAKES 4 SERVINGS
PREP: 10 MIN.

Not your average sundae, each sundae twists tradition by layering baked beans, coleslaw, barbecued pork, and, of course, a pickle on top.

DIVIDE 2 cups warm baked beans evenly among 4 small bowls, mugs, or glass jars. Top each portion of beans with ½ cup coleslaw and ¼ pound hot shredded barbecued pork. Serve sundae with a dill pickle wedge, if desired.

Make It Personal

Add a personal touch to each place setting with pretty name cards made of colorful cardstock or sturdy paper. Go a step further, and write an endearing message or include a recipe that you'll be serving for dinner. Then attach the cards to fresh herbs with ribbon, and tie them to chair backs or place them on the table. For party favors, wrap up a small package of a nonperishable ingredient from the recipe, such as rice, grits, or a dried herb, and place it with each card.

Complement a Natural Tablescape

Craft a rustic name card display stand from twigs. Take three clean twigs of equal length, and tie them tightly together at one end with twine, letting the opposite ends splay out to form three legs. Use a hot glue gun to attach a shorter twig horizontally between two legs, forming a miniature shelf on which the name card will sit. (Be sure the card fits on the shelf.) Decorate each stand with flowers or greenery. Continue the theme with a tablescape of small bouquets in ribbon-trimmed stemware.

recipe index

38

Miscellaneous

Salads and Dressings

91

Soups and Sandwiches

44

Vegetables and Side Dishes

Easy Party Solutions

At your next gathering, try these easy, eye-catching presentations.

And if things go awry, rely on the simple fixes below.

Marinated Olives

MAKES 8 SERVINGS

PREP: 20 MIN., CHILL: 8 HRS.

1 pound drained kalamata olives

12 pimiento-stuffed green olives, drained

12 pickled serrano or jalapeño peppers

¼ cup tequila

¼ cup lime juice

2 tablespoons orange liqueur

¼ cup minced fresh cilantro

1 teaspoon coarsely grated orange rind

STIR together all ingredients. Chill 8 hours.

◀ A martini glass makes a fun appetizer container for your guests to nibble from. Any type of glassware will work, so let creativity be your guide.

◀ Add style to guests' chairs with slender floral containers. Fill the cones with dried flowers, or if using seasonal blooms, use water picks to keep them fresh. At the end of the evening, each guest has a memento to take home.

▲ Choose green button-type Kermit mums for an unusual display. Florist foam balls are available in an assortment of sizes at many florists or grocery stores with a floral department. When surrounded with flowers, the balls appear almost twice their size. Soak the forms in a mixture of water and flower food diluted according to label directions. Cut stems about an inch under the bloom head. Push the stems into the form, with flowers touching or slightly overlapping, until the sphere is completely covered.

Top 10 Party Problem Solvers

Make the most of little mistakes with these tips.

- If cookies stick to a baking sheet, return them to the oven for 1 minute.
- If you've added too much salt to a soup, simply drop in a peeled, raw potato, and cook a few minutes. Then remove the potato before serving the soup.
- Make parfaits or a trifle out of dry cake layers or layers that fail to come out of pans evenly. Crumble the cake into glasses or a dish, and layer with fresh fruit and whipped cream.
- Cover an overly browned cake top with whipped cream or a sauce.
- Revive dry stuffing or dressing with a small amount of chicken broth.
- If chocolate "seizes" (clumps or hardens) while melting, try stirring a tablespoon of shortening or vegetable oil (per 6 ounces of chocolate) into the lumpy mixture and keep cooking over low heat.
- Moisten dry cookie dough with 1 to 2 tablespoons of milk.
- Clear up cloudy tea by adding a little boiling water.
- Restore crispness to limp salad greens by placing them in ice water, and refrigerating up to 1 hour. Drain well, wrap greens in paper towels, and refrigerate in plastic bags at least 4 hours.
- Rescue overbrowned biscuits by gently scraping the flat burned undersides against a fine-toothed grater. Do this over the sink—it's messy.